THE GODDESS IN THE SHADOW

LESSONS FROM THE DARK GODDESSES AND SHADOW WORK TO HARNESS DARK FEMININE ENERGY

ALLYCIA RYE

HENTOPAN
PUBLISHING

Illustrations by Gleiver Prieto

Book cover by Ivan Bjørn - www.ivanbjorn.com

CONTENTS

INTRODUCTION

We all have both a conscious and an unconscious mind. In this book, we will discuss and expand on the concept of the unconscious. Sigmund Freud was the first to pay attention to the unconscious mind and the significant role it plays in our motives, thoughts, personality and decisions. To more easily explain the difference between the conscious and unconscious, Freud used an illustration of an iceberg to show that the conscious mind is only that little tip above the water. Still, many of us think that the conscious mind is the most important part; the part that decides our personality and the trajectory of our lives. You might be surprised to hear that's not true. The unconscious part of our mind actually plays a major role in all aspects of our life.

Freud discovered that many significant and disturbing things about ourselves are hidden in our unconscious mind, sometimes put there to protect us. The problem is that whatever is in our unconscious has an effect on us, whether we're aware of it or not.

After Freud's initial work, Carl Jung came up with the idea of our shadow, a place in our unconscious where large parts of our true personality reside, parts that we must integrate into our subconscious if we are ever to be whole, complete human beings.

In this book we're going to delve deeper into what the shadow is, how it impacts us, and how to release what it holds so that we can be who we are truly meant to be. This work is called shadow work. When we do shadow work and glean insight into our unconscious, we begin to understand why we act the way we do. It is not easy; you may uncover painful and sometimes even traumatic experiences. But shadow work must be done, since it may be the most important work you will do in your entire life. My hope is that this book will help make that work easier for you.

Historically, dark feminine energy has been derided as witchcraft or evil. This has led to many people suppressing some of the most powerful parts of their personalities, pushing those aspects of the dark feminine deep into their shadow and causing significant problems in their lives. The bulk of this book is made up of introductions to ten dark goddesses from mythologies around the world, goddesses who hold wisdom from within the realm of that dark feminine energy. Each of the goddesses in this book hold lessons for us about our *own* dark feminine energy that we, both women and men, have hidden away in our shadow. They can teach us how to reclaim it from our shadow and integrate it with our conscious personalities. This book is a guide that will help you do that.

Each chapter starts with a story or myth about a particular goddess. We then learn about her history and the role she plays in the culture from where she originated. In each chapter you'll learn the lessons that the dark goddess can teach you, a ritual for you to begin to connect to your goddess guide, and a way to pull her from your shadow and evoke her in your daily life. This book uses the guidance of these powerful dark goddesses to help you in your shadow work as you reclaim your dark feminine energy and find your wholeness.

I came to write this book after a transformative experience in my own life. I had a problematic childhood, left suddenly parent-less and homeless at sixteen. Despite this, I finished high school and college and moved on with my life. I was soon married with two children, and had a good career. But through all of this I dealt with crippling anger, anger that I swallowed over and over again. I was a responsible woman, someone who controlled her feelings. I was not about to start shouting and throwing things. That was behavior for some wild, untamed person, not me.

Then I became sick. I had crippling back pain and sciatica. For four months, I could not sit or stand without incredible pain. I took bucketfuls of pain medicine. I had acupuncture. I went to chiropractors and physiotherapists. Nothing helped.

And then I met Pele, the goddess of fire and volcanoes. That was the most transformative experience of my life. Pele helped me to see the source of my physical pain— it was repressed anger. She guided me to a new place where I learned to look at my anger directly. If it was called for, I now allowed myself to become angry. I looked into my shadow and found that I was indeed a wild and untamed woman. And I was proud to be one! I had a right to be angry about my childhood. I had a right to be angry about my husband and children taking me for granted. I let all the anger out of my shadow, I let Pele's fire finish it completely, burning it all to ash, and I felt lighter, freer. I suddenly had so much creative power. On the other side of that transformative experience, I'm a new person, a pain-free person, and I'm so thankful for that. I now work with my collection of dark goddesses every day in my own personal shadow work.

After that experience, I began doing research into the other dark goddesses in this book. I knew I could not keep what I had learned to myself any more. Releasing the goddess Pele within me had set me free and healed me like nothing before had done. This was a secret I knew I had to share with others, so I wrote this book.

You can use this book as a handbook that you continually return to for guidance. For example, The Morrigan might be the guide you need for a few months. You'll do the ritual in her chapter and keep her symbols close. Then you might find Baba Yaga is calling you and you'll re-acquaint yourself with her chapter and perform her ritual to call her back to you. Then issues might arise that push you back to The Morrigan. In other words, this book can be used as needed, depending on your circumstances. Return to it when a dark goddess calls you, because you will most certainly hear them call you once you become acquainted with them. Shadow work is lifelong work, and my hope is that this book will help you be successful over and over again.

CHAPTER I
FACING YOUR SHADOW

F amed Swiss psychoanalyst and psychiatrist Carl Jung said that the personality is made up of three parts:

- The ego: our conscious mind that we are aware of and have control over.
- The personal unconscious: memories from our lives that we have suppressed.
- The collective unconscious: our inheritance from our ancestors that defines what it is to be human. You might think of it as the instinctual foundation for humanity.

The collective unconscious is made up of images and ideas that we share as members of the human race.

These images appear across cultures and time, in our fables and stories, in our art and in our dreams. Jung referred to the different parts of our collective unconscious as archetypes. There are an unlimited number of archetypes and these themes and images that define humanity are always increasing.

Jung identified four main archetypes from the collective unconscious. They are the persona, the anima/ animus, the self and the Shadow. One of these, the shadow, is what this book is about. It is only when we are aware of our shadow and the role it plays in our lives that we can begin to embrace it and finally integrate it with our ego to become a complete and whole person. We'll discuss this more later.

The four main archetypes give rise to Jung's twelve figurative archetypes that can be understood as figures that embody universal models of behavior.

THE TWELVE ARCHETYPES

Jung rejected the theory that a baby is born as a blank slate, or *tabula rasa*. The collective unconscious exists at birth as a sort of manual on how to be human. Each of the archetypes plays a role in the personality of all of us. Jung believed that the four main archetypes can intermingle and give rise to these twelve universal archetypes.

1. Ruler

The Ruler's main objective is to create successful and prosperous families and communities. They seek to control things and fear chaos and being pushed from the leadership position.

2. Artist

The Artist is creative and imaginative and wants to realize her vision. Her biggest weaknesses are perfectionism and fears mediocrity.

3. Sage

The Sage believes that the truth will set you free. She is searching for the truth and fears most that she might be mislead or duped.

4. Innocent

All the Innocent wants is to be happy. Her biggest fear is to be punished for being bad.

5. Explorer

The Explorer is on a mission to learn about herself by traveling and exploring the world. She wants freedom and fears that she may be trapped.

6. Rebel

The Rebel is all about liberation. She believes that rules were made to be broken. The Rebel may go too far and venture into criminality. She fears powerlessness.

7. Hero

The Hero is working towards mastery that will improve the world. She fears being vulnerable or weak.

8. Magician

The Magician is hooked on power and likes to make impossible things happen. She is most fearful of unintended negative consequences.

9. Jester

The Jester is all about the party. Finding pleasure and having a good time is the best way for the Jester to live her life. She fears being bored.

10. Every Man

The Every Man wants to belong. She wants to find a way to connect with everyone and fears being left out or somehow standing out in the crowd.

11. Lover

Intimacy is the most important thing for the Love. She wants to be surrounded by love. The problem comes is that she can be lost in that love and lose herself.

12. Caregiver

The Caregiver wants to be of service to others. She never wants to be seen as ungrateful or selfish.

Often one of the archetypes will dominate a personality, sometimes in a healthy way but other times in a less than healthy way. Knowing these archetypes can help you to begin to understand yourself.

One of the four main archetypes Jung focused on is the persona. The persona is the face that we show the world. This face changes, sometimes slightly, sometimes significantly, depending on where we are and who we are with. For example, I'm a slightly different person at work than I am when I'm at home or with my friends. I suspect this applies to almost all of us. Even amongst my friends, I can be a slightly different person with each of them. Maybe one of my friends loves football, so when I'm with her, I talk as if I love football and know a lot about it. Other parts of my personality might fall away. In this way, I'm showing her a persona rather than my true personality.

In some cases, this is quite healthy. For example, you don't want to be your "party animal persona" at your next job interview. On the other hand, if your persona takes over and you're no longer sure what your true personality is, this is unhealthy.

The other three of Jung's four main archetypes are the anima/animus, the self, and the shadow.

According to Jung, the anima is the totality of feminine qualities possessed by a male, while the animus comprises the male characteristics of a female personality. These are archetypes in our collective unconscious. All humans have either anima and animus as part of the inheritance from our ancestors.

The self is the archetype that we would all like to achieve. It is when our consciousness joins with our unconsciousness to create a unified personality. As we begin to identify as an individual, we also begin to separate from our collective unconscious. To achieve a unified self, as we grow, we are to constantly undergoing the process of merging the conscious and unconscious parts of our mind.

The shadow is one of the archetypes on which Jung focused a lot of attention, primarily because it can cause many psychological problems in our lives. The shadow is the dark side of our personality, the parts of ourselves that we would prefer stay hidden. According to Jung, "Everyone carries a shadow, the less it appears in the consciousness, the blacker and denser it is." To achieve a unified self, we must try to become aware of our shadow and to accept what is there, even if that acceptance is painful.

Let me give you an example. Celeste is married with two children. Her family is Christian and she was raised as a Christian. She would describe herself as a "good Christian wife and mother." At the same time, she often judges her divorced neighbor, who has numerous boyfriends and is not religious at all. Celeste believes that the way her neighbor is behaving is bad and also bad for her neighbor's son. Celeste's conscious mind, her ego, knows that she is a "good Christian wife and mother," but at the same time she is judging her neighbor. Is that a Christian way to behave? Her behavior is clashing with her self-description. To maintain her self-description, she must push all the parts of her personality that do not support her "good Christian wife and mother" self into her shadow. It would be hard for her to look at her judgment of her neighbor and accept that as a part of who she is, since that would make her self-description inaccurate.

How does our shadow affect us?

As Jung explains, "Until you make the unconscious conscious, it will direct your life and you will call it fate." In other words, the shadow contains things that we refuse to acknowledge are part of us, but if we do not work at becoming aware of it and how it impacts our consciousness and our personality, it will grow bigger and spill over in problematic ways.

As we grow and we act and react to our world and the people in it, we receive conscious and unconscious messages from our parents, friends and society. These messages tell us what the people around us value and what they do not. If we do things or believe things that they don't value, we will want to hide those thoughts and actions in our shadow so we will not be ridiculed or thought of as bad or wrong.

Often the shadow is seen as a place of evil, but it is not. It is merely a place where we keep parts of our personality that our ego or society deem unacceptable.

Let discuss another example. When Ann was a small girl, she was outgoing and quite talkative. She liked to put on shows for visitors where she danced and sang songs that she'd made up. Her mother was embarrassed by this and finally told Ann that "good girls" are quiet and don't perform for others that way. So Ann stopped. She put her love of dancing and singing in her shadow. She also put away her assertiveness and outgoing personality. She grew up to be a quiet, compliant woman. But even though she was quiet and compliant, a fury grew inside her. She was angry that people walked all over her. And she knew that anger was unacceptable in a "good girl," so she pushed that into her shadow too.

When Ann began to examine her shadow to see what was there, she discovered good, positive things about her personality. She could finally be creative and assertive because she recognized the judgments that had locked these traits in her shadow. One of the ways that our shadow affects us is that it can force our lives and our personalities to be smaller than they could be.

Our shadow keeps us apart from who we really are and all of the potential that is available to us.

The shadow causes a lot of fear as well. It also causes shame. We don't want to know what's in there in case it's terrible. And sometimes what's in there *is* terrible. We push trauma, often quite severe trauma, into our shadow so we don't deal with it and can go on living as if it never happened. This is why it takes courage and self-acceptance to begin to pull apart the many threads that are tangled up in our shadow.

The harsher our judgment and non-acceptance of the things that happen to us, the more fear and shame we will feel as we try to bring them to the awareness of our conscious mind. Take Reginald, for example. When he was seven, his father caught him masturbating and he was severely punished. His father also told his mother, and his mother became awkward with him from then on. There were no more hugs or cuddles on the sofa.

Reginald pushed this into his shadow. He learned that his penis and the sexual feelings he felt about it were evil. This had a profound effect on his sexual relationships because he believed that to include his sexuality in his conscious psyche meant the withdrawal of love, because that's what his mother had shown him.

Reginald's shadow was distorting his reality. Even when his wife tried to show him that sex was part of a loving relationship, he could not accept it. He was certain that it would cause her to withdraw her love as his mother had when she'd learned about him touching his penis. Until he began to become aware of what was happening in his shadow, he was certain that this was how the world worked.

Another important aspect of our shadow is that often what we hide in it; those aspects of our personality that we do not want to accept, we will project onto others. Tina is an academic, an expert in her field of study. Rob is a new professor in her department. During gatherings, Rob likes to talk extensively about his area of study. Tina views Rob as a pompous know-it-all. But the reality is that Tina is afraid that she herself can come off as a pompous know-it-all, though she has pushed that into her shadow. Her ego knows her as being humble. Tina is projecting onto Rob what she fears she herself might be, but she might be entirely wrong about Rob. He might simply be discussing his research, about which he is passionate, with others. Tina's projection distorts her reality.

Many, if not most, of our interpersonal conflicts can be traced back to our shadow. Much of it will stem from us projecting our fears of who we might be onto others and then making judgments about the person based on these projections. Though our conscious mind tells us we are taking in external information about what is happening, it is actually all coming from our own mind.

Remember Celeste? The other way our shadow affects us is it pushes us to live in self-deception. Perhaps Celeste is not a bad Christian, but, at the least, she is not the person she thinks she is or who she is trying so hard to be. That self-deception can take a lot of effort. It can generate many feelings, often negative ones, that pile up in our shadow until we are brave enough to turn our faces to them and begin to deal with the issues.

How can we find our own shadow?

You're probably wondering, if our shadow is hidden in our unconscious, how can we find it and begin to deal with the issues found there? Unfortunately, another problem is that our shadow is illusive; it tries to keep away from us.

When we try to be aware of the issues in our shadow, to recognise them, evaluate them, and accept them, this is called shadow work. Your ego tries to fight your shadow because the issues in the shadow threaten the story the ego is trying to tell you. Once the ego begins to accept the shadow, shadow work has begun. To become a unified self with a vibrant, complete personality that is engaged with the world, shadow work is imperative.

So, as we discussed earlier, if we pay close attention to people and instances that we judge harshly, we will almost certainly find a thread that takes us into our shadow. Perhaps you're someone who doesn't like weird, eccentric people. You have always fit in and you judge eccentric people harshly. Following that thread will likely lead you to be aware of the part of your shadow where you placed your fear that some aspects of your own personality might be deemed eccentric.

Another clue to finding your shadow is to pay attention to your emotions. What made you angry today? It's likely that whatever made you angry is something in yourself that you have disowned and put in your shadow. You won't do the shadow work there in the middle of the emotional storm, though, you'll do it later when you have time to reflect on it.

When you begin shadow work, here are some issues to keep in mind:

- Make sure you are in a calm, neutral place where you feel centered.
- Be compassionate with yourself. If you're someone who is used to feeling guilt and shame, try to set those feelings aside or else try to look at them differently. Accept who you are and show yourself compassion.
- Work hard to see yourself from a distance and cultivate self-awareness. Think about what happened, reflect on why things went the way they did. Be mindful of your actions and be non-judgmental.
- Forget good. No one is good. We are human, a mixture of good and bad and in-between.
- To do effective shadow work you must be brave and completely honest. No one likes to look at negative aspects of themselves, but you must be committed to being courageously honest.

THE BENEFITS OF INTEGRATING OUR SHADOW INTO OUR CONSCIOUSNESS

Once you begin to be conscious of the issues in your shadow, you will start to experience immediate bene-fits. Knowing your true self and unlocking all that has been held in your shadow will allow you to live more authentically with a clearer, more accurate view of the world and the people in it.

When you're less judgmental because you no longer project your own disowned characteristics onto others, your relationships will improve. You will unlock your empathy for others, compassion for yourself, and your wide-open creative mind. You will achieve maturity.

A surprising side benefit is increased energy and better physical health. Imagine now how you would feel if you could drop all of the shame and guilt-laden baggage that you have lugged around for years. That alone would be freeing. But more than that, there seems to be legitimate, scientifically-validated evidence that integrating your shadow with your ego has health benefits. Dr. John Sarno, a medical doctor and back expert, helped hundreds of people suffering from debilitating back pain by showing them that repressed anger, usually caused by that ego-pushed description of being good, was the actual cause of their pain. The anger in the unconscious - in the shadow - caused oxygen deprivation in cells and this produced real, authentic pain. Sometimes it was as easy as telling a patient what was happening and their pain disappeared. They were able to integrate unconscious anger into their consciousness. It was shadow work and it brought them back to health.

Our legacy from all of the humans who came before us includes the shadow that lives in our collective unconscious. We must not view it as an enemy to be battled, it is not. The shadow is a gift, like all of the archetypes, to help us navigate this human journey. The shadow is a product of living. It only becomes a problem when we close ourselves off from its potential. If we live mindfully, with compassion for ourselves and others, the shadow, once integrated into our conscious mind, becomes a guide to help us achieve our objectives and to become, finally, complete.

CHAPTER 2
THE DARK GODDESS WITHIN

In history and across cultures there are numerous stories about the dark goddesses. These dark goddesses are archetypes and part of our collective unconscious. The stories reflect that universality. The problem with the dark goddesses is that in a world ruled by men and religions formed by men, some of the strong feminine characteristics of dark goddesses are seen as a challenge to a patriarchal society. To protect the status quo, dark goddesses have been pushed into the universal shadow, cutting us off from their power.

That absence of the dark goddess energy and power in our psyche can be felt even if we do not feel that hurt consciously. It's not surprising that most of us are moving in the world with wounds that cannot heal and hurts that we project onto others. We've been cut off from integral parts of who we are meant to be and we are fractured because of it. We cannot begin to heal until we go searching for our missing pieces and reinstate them to where they belong.

We've learned already that Jung taught us we must pull our shadow into the light if we are ever to become whole, healed, mature beings. If this is to happen, the dark goddesses need to emerge from the shadows and become part of who we are.

THE MIS-DEFINITION OF DARK

In our popular culture, dark is most often aligned with bad and evil things. This is a misinterpretation of darkness. In Jung's work, the shadow is a place of darkness, but it is not a place to be feared, nor is it a place where things are judged as evil. It is only that part of ourselves that's not yet revealed. It is the place where we put aspects of ourselves that do not align with our ego, memories of experiences that might be difficult for us to understand and accept, and parts of our true self that the culture we live in does not appreciate.

If we think of water in a lake, the surface might be full of the light coming from the sun. But as we begin to go deeper, it becomes darker. In that darkness is where life is, the fish and plants, the life-giving plankton. When we go into the dark, we begin to understand better what a lake is. In the Song of Solomon in the Bible, darkness does not mean evil, it means wisdom. Darkness means deep and not on the surface. To venture into the dark is to gain wisdom and to find hidden answers.

Of course, some of what is in our shadow is painful, and might sometimes even be judged as evil. In most religions, we are taught that evil and sin are bad and full of shame. We must avoid these things, repress them if they are part of us. This is a patriarchal, masculine way of attending to these natural feelings. We push them down into the darkness, a darkness into which we must never venture. Perhaps this is why darkness is seen in the way that it is in our culture.

Jung had a more feminine, inclusive way of dealing with these painful issues. He did not tell people to hide them, he advised people instead to step into that darkness, to embrace it, and to incorporate what they learn there into their conscious selves.

The rejection of the dark goddesses is part of that patriarchal, masculine ethos. It is neither healthy nor helpful. The dark goddesses teach us lessons and have qualities that show us the profound wisdom of the feminine psyche. It is all there in our universal unconsciousness, in that wise darkness.

INDIVIDUATION

Before we go further, we need to take a moment to fully understand Jung's term 'individuation'. In the last chapter, we started to learn about shadow work, that practice of bringing into the light of our conscious mind those unconscious thoughts in our shadow.

Becoming aware of what is in our shadow is only part of the work. Integrating those aspects into our personality is called individuation. We are merging all parts of ourselves to become the psychologically whole, mature, and wise person we were always meant to be. When we begin the process of individuation, our healing begins. Individuation, though, requires courage if we are to be successful. As Jung said:

"The shadow is a moral problem that challenges the whole ego personality, for no one can become conscious of the shadow without considerable moral effort. To become conscious of it involves recognising the dark aspects of the personality as present and real. This act is the essential

condition of any self-knowledge, and it therefore, as a rule, meets with considerable resistance."

Our moral courage will be called upon even more once we begin the journey to meet the dark goddesses in our shadow and welcome them into our lives, because in many ways it is not only our ego that is trying to stop us from meeting them, but the culture and society in which we live. The resistance will be strong. We must walk bravely into this task of reclaiming ourselves.

WHO ARE THE DARK GODDESSES?

The dark goddesses named in the rest of this book come from the stories and myths of cultures around the world. Though they originate in diverse cultures, they have many things in common.

The dark goddesses are universally independent women. They do not reduce themselves when society attempts to force them to; instead they rise up and confront those efforts to control them. They are unrestrained; they are proud.

The dark goddesses you will learn about in this book have extraordinary, magical powers over sexuality, transformation, death, and rebirth. They teach us how to face the challenges that we encounter on our life's journey in a way that is transformative and that empowers and reaffirms us. The dark goddesses' powers live in us, and are simply waiting to be rediscovered.

HOW WILL THE DARK GODDESSES HELP US?

The dark goddesses are about the destruction of the paradigms and myths that we have consciously and unconsciously absorbed as part of our personality and psyche, but that are not serving us. They show us that what we think is a fact actually is not. That what we have relied on as a certainty never was certain.

Honestly, this process will be frightening. All destruction is scary in some ways, especially when that dismantling involves the foundation upon which we have built our personality. We must prepare ourselves for that fear. We must let go of the conscious and unconscious actions, reactions, fears and emotions that we have developed since we were small children but which no longer serve us. The dark goddesses will help us to do that. Once we become aware of and remove these unhealthy ideas that repress us, we will begin to see that we never really needed them at all, even though we held onto them with a white-knuckle grip, as if they were our saviours.

What we need to keep in mind at all times is that we are on a journey to enlightenment and awakening. We are searching for the rest of ourselves so we can finally be whole. This is paramount if we are to heal and become who we are destined to be.

Let's look at an example of how a dark goddess helped Jennifer. Jennifer was married to Greg for nineteen years. She was sure that she knew herself, knew her husband, and knew the path her life was on. Jennifer worked at home, taking care of their home and children. Greg travelled a lot for his job in the pharmaceutical industry. Jennifer and Greg had a good life. A nice home, two teenage daughters about to finish high school and go on to college. Jennifer was content, if a bit fearful of going out into the world on her own, but that didn't matter, since she never needed to do it.

Then her world fell apart. Greg wanted a divorce. He was no longer in love with her. In a conversation that lasted less than thirty minutes, Jennifer's entire life and the person she was certain she was collapsed. The woman she knew to be Jennifer disappeared into the ether with all of society's expectations and constraints. She wondered who she was now.

At first, she fought everything. She was angry and depressed. She was frightened. Then one night in a dream she was visited by Hecate, one of the dark goddesses. She woke the next day and rushed to her computer to learn more about Hecate.

When Jennifer's attention shifted to the message Hecate held for her, the dark goddess within her began to emerge and light filled the heavy darkness around her. Hecate showed her that change was mandatory on our journey, not something to be feared. Yes, it was often painful, but that didn't mean we should try to avoid it. Hecate insisted that embracing the change in its entirety was the only way to discover the new understanding and awakening that could be found on the other side.

Jennifer made a quiet place in the corner of her bedroom where she could meditate on the lessons Hecate wanted her to pull into her life. She let go and let the change happen. Soon she became optimistic about her future. She didn't yet know what was on the other side, but she had a new awareness and was grateful for the change: the death of her previous life and the birth of her new one. Hecate gave her new hope and agency in her life.

In some ways this journey is dangerous. We will change during this process and some people in our lives will not like those changes. Not everyone liked Jennifer after she changed. As she found agency in her life, some people around her felt threatened. They didn't like this new Jennifer, who was strong and brave and willing to take chances on her own. They tried to force their status quo thinking on her They tried to tell her she was not up to the new challenges, that she should look for another husband to take care of her. Occasionally this caused Jennifer to question her dark goddess guide and to undermine her own abilities, but even though she had some doubts and fears about the unknown ahead of her, she steadied herself and continued.

Fear of the destruction of what we were and what we believed, and the wobbly feeling that reality may not be exactly what we thought it was, will be the price we pay to reveal the dark goddesses and tap into the stores of creative and personal energy they hold.

The dark goddesses have been with us in ancient myths for centuries, and have been within us for just as long. Each of the goddesses represents a part of our personality yet to be revealed. That ancient wisdom has been hidden from us, but we will now begin to uncover it in the heroic process of rediscovery.

LETTING THE DARK GODDESSES GUIDE YOU

The dark goddesses are not just for women, but for all of us. Despite the stories popular culture tells us, men are only complete if they have tapped into their feminine energy, even more so when they uncover the power of the dark goddesses within. Some choose one of the dark goddesses as their personal deity and worship them, but this is not required to benefit from their guidance. It's not necessary to be part of any particular religion in order to learn the lessons from the dark goddesses.

Each coming chapter will focus on one of the dark goddesses, and will begin with a story or myth about that goddess. Stories and myths give us the clearest and simplest view of the goddess' archetypes. We'll look first at those myths and the lessons they teach us, and then examine the rituals and daily practices that can help us evoke the dark goddess inside us. I recommend setting up an area where you can go to think and meditate on each of the goddesses, and summon them into your consciousness. The chapters will offer ideas about how to set up these areas and will provide some practices and rituals that will assist you in summoning the dark goddesses into your consciousness.

Our shadow, in many ways, is a personification of these wild, free, dark goddesses that embrace and revere every aspect of their femininity. So why don't we meet them?

CHAPTER 3
SEDNA

In Inuit mythology, Sedna was a beautiful young woman with many suitors, but none of them were acceptable to her. Her widowed father searched day and night to find a husband who his stubborn daughter would agree to marry. He was growing old and needed a son-in-law to help him fish and hunt.

One day, her father watched with frustration as one of the most handsome men on the island was sent away by Sedna, rejected like all the others before him. She sat calmly combing her hair and smiling. Her father became furious.

"My daughter, tell me what was wrong with that one? He's strong, a good hunter. He would make a good husband," her father declared.

"Who said I want a husband like that?" Sedna asked.

"You must marry someone! If you can't make up your mind, I'll choose your husband for you."

"You don't need to worry," Sedna said. "I'll know my husband when I see him."

A month later, a strange masked man appeared. He wooed Sedna, telling her of the beautiful bear skins she would sleep on and the delicious meat she would eat from the animals he would hunt for her. Within a few days she fell in love with him and agreed to marry him. Her father was relieved.

But to Sedna's surprise, after they were married, the man revealed that he was a fulmar, which is a sea bird! He was a bird who could pose as a man. He had tricked her!

Despite his deception, Sedna went to live on another island with him and the other sea birds. They lived in his dirty nest filled with stinking parts of dead fish, dirty feathers and sharp sticks. Sedna was very unhappy.

After a few months, her father came to visit her and saw how unhappy she was. They attempted to escape and in the process her father killed her bird husband.

"Come, Sedna! Run quickly! The other fulmars will be angry when they find out what I have done!" her father shouted as they ran for his boat.

Sedna and her father got to the middle of the sea and thought they were safe. But suddenly the fulmars arrived and, in their anger, conjured up a deadly storm. The wind blew and the waves grew bigger and bigger. The birds flew around and around the boat, causing it to rock dangerously. Sedna's father feared that the boat would capsize and decided that the best thing he could do was give the birds what they wanted, so he threw Sedna over the side.

Sedna managed to grip the edge of the boat to stop herself from drowning. "No, Father! Why are you doing this to me?" she cried into the mighty wind.

Her father said nothing but instead grabbed his fishing knife and chopped off Sedna's fingers. Sedna could not believe that her father could betray her so mercilessly.

She began to sink to the bottom of the sea. In her fury, as she fell and fell, she changed from a mortal into an immortal goddess. Her fingers swam off and became the fish, seals, dolphins, whales and all the other animals of the ocean.

From then on, Sedna, the Goddess of the Sea, lived on the ocean floor. Her top half was still the beautiful woman Sedna, but her bottom half had transformed into a whale tail. Because she has no fingers, her hair grows long and tangled. The sea animals regularly get caught in the knots in her hair. When they do, the humans at the surface, including her father, suffer, because they cannot find anything in the sea to eat, since it's all caught in Sedna's hair.

The humans learn that if they want to survive, they must appease Sedna. She demands that they respect her. They choose a shaman who can sing and this person must swim deep into the ocean's depths through Sedna's guards and other dangers. Once at Sedna's lair, the shaman must sing sweetly while massaging the goddess, and carefully untangle her hair, then comb it lovingly. It is only when she is calm and feels respected that she releases all of the fish and seals and whales back into the sea and the people can have food again.

THE HISTORY OF SEDNA

The Inuit people live across the northern Arctic parts of the world in Alaska, Canada and Greenland. Sedna is considered the Mother of the Sea and is one of their most important deities. She is called by various names across the area. For example, in parts of Greenland she is called Arnaqquassaaq, but in other places she is called Taleelsyu, which means the great leader of the underworld, or Arnapkapfaaluk, meaning the Big Bad Woman.

The myth of Sedna is one of the creation myths of the Inuit people. Even now they know that to have a successful fishing or hunting season in the sea, when the first animal is caught, a piece of its liver must be thrown back into the water to appease and thank Goddess Sedna. When Sedna is not respected, she creates deadly storms and keeps the sea animals in her hair. The myth also reminds the Inuits to respect everything in the sea and the natural world.

Symbols related to Sedna include sand, representations of sea animals, shells and water.

SEDNA'S LESSONS FOR US

Betrayal is a difficult part of life that many of us experience, and it's made worse when the one betraying us is someone who we thought loved us. It can send us into a downward spiral of depression that can be difficult to come out of. It is a hurt that goes to the deepest part of our soul. Many of us have also likely been in situations in which we have been disrespected, especially as women. Where our voices and our power have been marginalized and treated as unimportant. This is why we can embrace Sedna as an appropriate guide and teacher.

Dark Goddess Sedna teaches us two important lessons. As she sank into the dark water, a metaphor for the unconscious, after the trauma of her bird husband lying to her and then her father's betrayal, she found transformation, changing from a mortal to a god. She transformed into her true, powerful self. She teaches us that a time of darkness will be a time of transformation. But also that we must take that painful journey into our unconscious if we are ever going to learn the important lessons there that can change us.

Sedna is a perfect goddess to evoke when we are sinking into the deep, dark places. She teaches us that from that darkness will come our true light, so we need not be fearful. She is our ally during those frightening times of our lives.

Sedna also teaches us that we must be respected. If those around us neglect to respect us, we should insist that they do. Sedna demands respect, and if she doesn't get it, she withholds the food for the people and creates violent storms until they learn who she is and respect her worthiness. We, too, are worthy of respect, even if others suggest we are not—*we know who we are.* If others do not know yet, then we need to teach them our lessons by showing them our storms.

A RITUAL FOR SEDNA

As I said, Sedna is an excellent goddess to call on when you're feeling as if you're sinking into your own depths or when you've been betrayed or hurt by someone as Sedna was. Performing the ritual to summon her is a way to integrate into the rest of your psyche the parts of your shadow that Sedna represents.

Sedna lives in the cool darkness of the sea, surrounded by the ocean's music, so we need to create a similar environment for her to feel welcomed.

What you will need for this ritual:

- Music of sea sounds, either waves or the songs of sea mammals like whales
- Essential oils, including lime, rosemary, eucalyptus, and lavender

- Shells, sand, water and rock salt
- A small blue or green bowl
- Your journal

First you need to make ocean essential oil. This is made with:

- Eight drops of lime essential oil
- Six drops of lavender essential oil
- Two drop of eucalyptus essential oil
- Two drop of rosemary essential oil

On a small table in a quiet place, spread out the sand in a circle. On the edges of the circle, place the shells. In the middle of the circle put the blue or green bowl, which will represent the sea, and fill it about a quarter of the way with rock salt, then fill it to the top with water.

Turn on the ocean music. Rub some of the ocean essential oil on your forehead at your third eye. Pour the rest of the essential oil into the bowl in the middle. Close your eyes. Breathe deeply for four counts on the inhale, four counts holding, and four counts on the exhale. Repeat this many times until you feel thoroughly relaxed and focussed on your breath.

Keep your eyes closed, still breathing deeply, and visualize yourself entering the sea. Feel the cool water on your feet. Feel it rise up your legs as you walk further into the water. Then dive in. Feel the cool water embracing your body. You are able to breathe freely under the water. You are swimming deeper and deeper. You see fish and corals of all colors. Seals and whales swim past you. You see a big green sea turtle. You are part of the sea now. Feel it.

Visualize Goddess Sedna appearing in all of her mighty glory. She is smiling; she's been waiting for you. She welcomes you to her world. Pick a few pieces of the rock salt with the essential oil and rub them around in your hands as you chant softly for a few minutes:

Mother of the Sea I am here for your blessings.
Mother of the Sea I am here for your wisdom.

See Goddess Sedna opening your channel to your internal wisdom; the deep, inherited wisdom of your ancestors. She is releasing your power within. Feel it. Let it retake its rightful place in your consciousness and in your body.

Feel her safe welcoming spirit surrounding you. There is nothing to fear. Ask her to help you on your journey:

Goddess Sedna, Mother of the Sea, support me as I pass through this darkness. Lead me to the light. Show me my power.

Sit in silence listening to the sea sounds you've chosen. Slowly emerge from the sea. Visualize yourself swimming up to the surface. See the sunlight above you through the water. Then feel yourself standing with the water covering your feet. Feel the warm sun on your face. Slowly walk out of the sea. Finally stand on the beach and open your eyes. How do you feel?

Immediately write about how you feel in your journal. Do not worry about sentences or grammar. Write quickly for two minutes and then close your journal. Leave your meditation area and do something else.

After an hour or so, return to your meditation area, and write in your journal about your complete experience. Write what you felt, how you think you will change now, and about your interactions with Goddess Sedna. How do you think she has helped you?

It's good to begin this ritual practice when you have the time and space to repeat it for a few days in a row. This is the best way to gain the benefits. Then every time you are passing through a dark period or when those around you seem to be disrespecting your power, do this ritual again.

EVOKING THE GODDESS SEDNA

If the lessons of Goddess Sedna are the ones most needed in your life at the moment, you will want to keep her present as much as possible throughout your day. One way is to keep the colors of the sea, the blues and greens, on your body, either in your clothing or in an accessory like a scarf. This will continually remind you of your guide.

Preparing amulets to keep on you at all times is also helpful. They can act a bit like a fast track to your psyche when you hold them in your hand. These might include small vials of sea water or sand, a silver sea bird, whale or a Sedna pendant, even a shell. You might also read more about the mythology around the Goddess Sedna. You should keep a bottle of prepared ocean essential oil handy. Rub a bit into your third eye and your throat chakra at the base of your throat. This too will keep Sedna in your conscious mind.

Once you are aware of the lessons each dark goddess can teach you, your psyche will turn to them when they are required. Being aware of what you are experiencing will also teach you when need each goddess. Pay attention to when Sedna comes into your consciousness. Be aware of what is happening to you at these times. Write about it in your journal. Eventually you should be able to use the lessons Sedna teaches you to empower yourself at those vulnerable times.

Water and the sea are metaphors for your unconscious. In your shadow work where you dive into your unconscious, Sedna is a perfect dark goddess to be your ally and your guide. She understands pain, betrayal, death and rebirth, and she understands how to use that pain, and the inevitable resulting anger, in a positive way to empower us and help us to merge her archetype into our personality.

CHAPTER 4
THE MORRIGAN

The Goddess Morrigan first appeared to the warrior Cúchulainn when he was defending his town, Ulster, against an attack by the army of Connaught, led by Queen Maeve.

One day before he entered the battle, the Morrigan attempted to seduce Cúchulainn by offering herself to him, but he refused her advances and dismissed her, despite her great beauty.

Enraged at being rejected, the Morrigan used her shape-shifting powers to transform into an eel so she could swim up to Cúchulainn and trip him as he made his way through a fjord to return to the battle. But Cúchulainn managed to punch the eel and break its rib. Soon after, a gray wolf appeared, driving a herd of cattle toward him but Cúchulainn took out his slingshot and was able to blind the wolf in one eye, stopping her. But his problems were not over. The Morrigan then transformed into one of the cows leading the stampede. Cúchulainn used his slingshot once again, and the heifer went down with a broken leg, forcing the Goddess to accept defeat.

Cúchulainn returned to the battle in time to help the army claim victory. They chased the invaders off and Ulster was safe again.

As Cúchulainn headed home in a victorious mood, he came upon an old woman milking her cow, who said to him, "You have saved us, Cúchulainn. Come let me give you some milk as a thank you."

The old woman was blind in one eye, had a broken leg and seemed to have trouble with her ribs, but weary from battle, Cúchulainn didn't notice any of this. He stopped and took the cup of milk. He took three sips, and with each sip, he blessed her. "Woman, thank you for this. May you be blessed for your kindness," he said.

Cúchulainn didn't notice that each of his blessings had healed each of the old woman's injuries, and before his eyes, the old woman became the Morrigan and disappeared.

The Goddess would appear once more before Cúchulainn shortly before the mighty warrior's death. As he was on his way into yet another battle, he came upon an old woman in the fjord washing bloodied body armour. This was a very bad omen to see before a battle, but Cúchulainn nevertheless proceeded to join his fellow warriors in battle.

During the battle, Cúchulainn was struck a mortal wound, but in an attempt to terrify the enemy and hold them back, he pulled himself to a nearby tree, to which he bound himself with his own intestines. Finally a black crow landed on his shoulder and he drifted off to sleep forever, revealing his death to the enemy.

THE HISTORY OF THE MORRIGAN

The Morrigan, from Irish mythology, is the Goddess of War. Sometimes she is seen as three, which is a very important number in Irish mythology. She might be three sisters: Badb, Macha and Nemain, or she might be represented by three animals: the cow, crow, and wolf, as we learned from the above story about her encounters with the great warrior Cúchulainn.

She is a shape-shifter and is able to win on any battlefield because of that power. Her shape-shifting ability connects her deeply to the natural world. She is the goddess of prophecy and fate. She represents illusions and the hidden. She is a warrior and defends women and children, especially.

The Irish believe that if you come upon the Morrigan washing blood-stained clothes, your death is near.

There are numerous places in Ireland that celebrate the Morrigan, including the Cave of the Morrigan, also called The Cave of the Cats, which is said to have been her home and the entrance to the Other World.

Symbols associated with the Morrigan include: red wine, milk, crow and raven feathers, figurines of wolves, crows or cows, and red clothing.

THE MORRIGAN'S LESSONS FOR US

We sometimes meet people who we feel instinctively could cause us harm in some way if we reveal ourselves completely to them. They are judgmental. They hold tightly to cultural rules, religious doctrine, or societal dictates that we know are not part of who we truly are. To let these people see a side of us that contradicts any of that could be dangerous. They might judge us, reject us or ridicule us. As a result, we unconsciously hide our true selves from them as a protective mechanism. We make ourselves smaller when we feel that the other person cannot see or understand who we truly are, or when they dismiss us out of hand as being unimportant. Because of our past experiences with such people, because of these wounds that they've left behind inside of our psyche, we've hidden powerful parts of our true personality in our shadow. We get stuck in one form, often a cowering, fearful form, so as to not experience the harm of rejection and dismissal.

The Morrigan appeared to Cúchulainn and he dismissed her as a nuisance. He undermined who she truly was. He was unable to recognize her immense feminine power and treated her rudely. The Morrigan showed him time and again that her power should be able to be seen no matter what form she took, but Cúchulainn was too arrogant and preoccupied to recognize it.

The Morrigan teaches us the incredible feminine power of shape-shifting, if we use it correctly. We're extremely powerful and we should be recognized as such. Reach deep into your shadow and take back your ability to change forms whenever the situation calls for it. You can hide in another form or you can reveal yourself in your full magnificence. But only the worthy should be gifted with your true glorious self.

When you transform and begin to reclaim the elements of your personality locked in your shadow, others may fear the power you have that they have not yet been able to reclaim for themselves. They will not be ready for you. Once you learn the Morrigan's lesson you will be able to consciously choose those around you who are worthy of the true, empowered you. You will leave the others in their ignorance; they will have to do their own shadow work before they can see the truth.

A RITUAL FOR THE MORRIGAN

The Morrigan's ritual, like all the rituals in this book, will help you focus your attention on the lessons that the dark goddess is teaching you, so you can pull into your conscious mind those characteristics the lessons cultivate. You will be able to incorporate them with your conscious personality and therefore move closer to your true and complete self.

With the cultivation of your self-awareness, you'll begin to uncover which dark goddess you require at which stage of your life. This will change as circumstances change. You might need the Morrigan today, but once you've learned her lesson, you might move on. Then something happens that makes you want to return to the Morrigan. Life is constantly throwing us curve balls, right? We may think we've dealt with our ability to shape-shift when needed and then quickly reinstate our true selves, but then someone comes along who pushes us back inside our shadow, and we find we're unable to shape-shift back to our true selves. You need only return to the Morrigan and practice this ritual to get back on track again.

What you will need for this ritual:

- Three red candles
- Sandalwood essential oil
- A half glass of milk
- A half glass of red wine (if you are unable to drink alcohol, replace with red juice)
- Calming instrumental music

Find a quiet space in your home. It would be helpful to have a small table on which you can place the things you need. Sit on the floor in front of the table, in any way that is comfortable for you. You might sit on a blanket, cushion or a yoga mat.

Place the three candles in a triangle and light them. Turn on the music at a soft level. To begin to calm your thoughts, dab three dots of sandalwood oil on your third eye. This will open you to be receptive to the Morrigan's power and assistance.

Close your eyes. Listen to the music and attempt to clear your mind of thoughts. Let the music flow over you.

When your mind is calm, envision the Morrigan as an old woman. She is handing you a glass of milk. Drink your milk in three sips. Thank her. With each sip, think of a wound inside of you caused by someone who dismissed your power. See the milk heal the wound. Let the energy of the wound go, watch it disappear into the air.

Go back to listening to the music with your eyes closed. Place both your hands at your solar plexis chakra just below your breasts. This is the center of your confidence. Feel the Morrigan bolstering your confidence. Feel her giving you complete control of your life. Feel that chakra opening and feel yourself as a confident person, a person who knows and loves herself.

Now sip the wine in three sips. With the first sip, envision yourself as a wolf. You are free to be exactly who you are. You are fierce. You are powerful. Feel yourself completely as a wolf.

With your next sip, envision yourself as a crow. You are rising in the air. You see everything. You know everything. You are buoyant and full of joy. You are free to be completely yourself.

With the last sip, see yourself. Look into the shadow and pull out the pieces of you that are hiding. Be proud of them. Let each piece build you, make you bigger and more powerful. You are a powerful goddess. Feel yourself. Know yourself. Love yourself.

Put both of your hands back on your solar plexis. Close your eyes and let all that the ritual has given you take its place in your body. Open your eyes and blow out the candles. Before blowing out each candle, express your gratefulness to the Morrigan.

EVOKING THE MORRIGAN

When you are approaching a situation where you might find yourself retreating instead of shape-shifting and you need to evoke the Morrigan within you, there are a few things you can do. If you can find a small figurine of a wolf, crow or cow, it would be useful to keep them nearby. Holding one in your hand will remind you of the confidence you gained in the ritual and of the characteristics that you want to remain firmly in your consciousness. Wearing red, or keeping red items around you will also help keep the Morrigan near.

The Warrior Goddess is an important one to evoke and to rely on during shadow work. She helps us reclaim our power and reminds us who is worthy of our true selves. Come back to her often.

CHAPTER 5
HECATE

One day Persephone, daughter of Zeus and Demeter, Goddess of Agriculture, was out collecting flowers with her friends. In the distance, she spotted the most beautiful flower she had ever seen. She left her friends and went to pick the yellow blossom of the narcissus flower, but as she reached down to pluck it, a great hole opened up in the earth and Hades, the god of the Underworld, appeared in his chariot.

Hades had fallen in love with the beautiful girl and pulled her into the chariot, vowing to make her his wife. Persephone screamed but no one came to help her. Persephone looked behind her and saw the light disappear as the hole closed and she was sure her old life was lost to her forever.

When Persephone did not return from picking flowers, her mother, Demeter, was devastated. For nine days and nights Demeter searched the world for her daughter, but to no avail. On the tenth day, Hecate came to Demeter, holding a torch in both hands, and told her that she had heard Persephone screaming when Hades had carried her to the Underworld. She had waited nine days to reveal what she knew so that both mother and daughter might have the chance to understand what it felt like to be apart and to complete their own individual journey. Now, though, Hecate offered to take Demeter to the Underworld to bring her daughter back.

Hecate not only had the torches to guide them, Demeter was surprised to find that she had the keys to the gate that stood between Earth and the Underworld. She unlocked it and they passed through. On the other side they found that Hades had already married Persephone.

"Please," Demeter begged, seeing how sad her daughter was, "Persephone is not meant to live in the Underworld. Let her return to Earth with me."

After much begging and pleading, Hades finally relented. He agreed that Persephone could live on Earth for six months, but must return to the Underworld for the other six months of the year. Hecate became Persephone's companion, guiding her back and forth across the boundary between the two worlds.

THE HISTORY OF HECATE

Hecate is one of the most important dark goddesses we will meet when it comes to our shadow work. She plays a major role in Greek mythology, but in fact she originated even before the gods on Mount Olympus. She is a Titan. Her parents were Persis and Asteria. It is thought that that the Asterian Mountain range on the island of Crete is named after Hecate's mother Asteria.

After the battle between the Olympians and the Titans, all of the Titans, including Hecate's parents, were banished to the Underworld except for Hecate because she had helped Zeus.

Hecate is the goddess of crossroads, especially where three roads cross. She is a liminal goddess, straddling boundaries between the accepted and the unconventional, the conscious and the unconscious, the light and the dark, life and death. She is able to guide and shine light into the darkness, which is why she was able to guide Demeter through the Underworld to Hades. She is closely associated with the three phases of the moon: waxing, waning and the dark moon.

Hecate is most often depicted as either having three complete bodies or three heads on one body, each looking in another direction. She is usually accompanied by dogs and is always holding her two torches.

In ancient times, she was a household goddess. Pillars called Hecataea stood in doorways to homes, shrines, and even cities, at the border, to protect the owners from evil. There was a major shrine to Hecate in Phrygia and Caria in ancient Greece and cults worshipped her.

Her symbols include: black dogs, keys, torches, serpents, crossroads and the dark moon.

HECATE'S LESSONS FOR US

When we're doing shadow work, Hecate is one of the most important dark goddesses to ask for assistance. She carries the torch to light our way so we can feel safe as we make our journey into the darkness. She also holds the keys to unlock any obstacles or gates along the way. She was a loyal guide to Persephone and she can be a loyal guide to you.

We know already that shadow work is a lifelong commitment that can be frightening and disorientating. The frightening part of our journey is not the beginning or the end, but the transition. Hecate lives in those transitions, she is the goddess of the liminal spaces, where we are neither here nor there, but in that unsettling middle. She holds the keys to help us pass with ease. She holds the torch to light our way. Her lesson is not to be afraid in those transitions. We should embrace them because they are the paths we need to arrive at our destination.

Most of us can think of times when we have hesitated to act or move because of fear. Whether it was literally in the dark, like walking to our car in a parking lot at night or entering a dark room where we heard a noise, or something less literal but still full of darkness, we've all experienced such situations. Maybe you lacked knowledge or felt unworthy. Maybe you feared making an important decision about your life and hesitated. These hesitations are normal. Sometimes, though, they can keep us stuck. We're unable to walk into that darkness and this stops our progress. If we cannot walk through that dark parking lot, we cannot get to our car and go home. If we're afraid to apply for the job we want for fear of rejection, or if we're afraid to leave a relationship that is no longer serving us because we don't know if we can survive alone, then we stop our lives when they are meant to move forward. We lose the opportunity of growth and a new awareness about ourselves.

We cannot be successful with the process of our individuation unless we transform. When we do, on the other side we will find compassion, new awareness, and understanding. We must take those first steps and begin the journey if we are ever to reach that other side where our true self awaits us.

The metaphor of Hecate's torches cannot go unnoticed by people like us who are in the midst of our shadow work. We know our shadow is the dark place where we put what our ego does not want us to see. We are not sure what we might find there, and that is where the apprehension about it comes into being. When light is shown on our shadow and we are able to see what is there, that's when we begin the journey to make those important dark aspects of our psyche part of our consciousness. Hecate's lesson is that there is nothing to fear.

A RITUAL FOR HECATE

Hecate is a major goddess. It is important when we want to ask her for assistance that we approach her with the correct respect. Begin with an offering. You should make your first attempt to request assistance from Hecate during the dark phase of the moon.

What you will need for this ritual:

- Myrrh and frankincense incense
- Honey, pomegranate, and an onion

This offering should be made at night. If possible, try to do your ritual near a tree, especially a willow or a dark yew tree. If you don't have one of these types of trees available to you, then put your offering at the base of any tree, but ideally one to which you have an attachment. Light the incense sticks and push them into the ground apart from each other. Place your offerings between the incense.

Sit in front of your offerings, close your eyes and calm your mind with deep cleansing breaths at a count of four for your inhalation, hold the breath for four, and then exhale for four. Do this at least five times, or more if your mind is too busy.

When you are calm, create a vision of Hecate in your mind, a beautiful goddess with long dark flowing hair, carrying her torches, surrounded by her many black dogs. Then ask her for her assistance.

Goddess Hecate, I humbly come before you to help me on my journey. Help me find my way through the darkness and into the light. I ask for your assistance.

Stay for at least five minutes, repeating your request in between deep breathing. For the last two minutes sit quietly.

In the coming days and weeks, be aware of anything that may be a message from Hecate. Often she will come to you in a dream, so pay attention to your dreams. But she may also send a message to you in your daily life. Did a black dog pass by? Did you see an owl, the universal messenger? Were there keys in your dream? Was there a serpent?

For the next two weeks, each night go out to the tree where you left the offerings, even if they are now gone. Light incense and sit and perform your calm breathing. Clear your mind. Think of nothing. Meditate. Do not call her to you, she will come.

During this time, continue writing in your journal. Continue doing your shadow work. In the days that follow opening yourself up to Hecate, if you are working on releasing aspects of yourself from your shadow, an opportunity may appear in your life that will seem like a problem. Hecate has put it before you. It will not be anything major, but it will be something that you don't want to do, something you're uncomfortable doing, though you may not be able to say why. Hecate has presented this for you to shed light on a bit of darkness. It is a slight push to get you to face something in your shadow that you have been avoiding. Do the thing that makes you feel uncomfortable. She is using her wisdom to assist you. Accept it. She is now acting as your guide.

In your journaling about this uncomfortable situation that you pushed yourself into, try to see what part of your personality, hidden in your shadow, may have played a role in this. When you find it, thank Hecate with an offering like the offering you made on the first night.

EVOKING HECATE

There will be days as you work on integrating the conscious and unconscious parts of your psyche when you will feel blocked, as if something is not allowing you to make progress. You will need Hecate on those days to unlock those gates and guide you through.

Keeping a key on a string or chain around your neck will remind you that Hecate is already there. She has empowered you to open those gates and go into those dark places. Whenever you come to a crossroads, envision her. Another way to keep her close is to recognize her spirit in the willow trees you pass or the dogs at the park. Close your eyes and know that she is there, not only outside of you, but within.

In our shadow work, in our journey toward a new awareness, we will be frightened to cross that boundary from the light into darkness; it's natural. Hecate is the dark goddess that we need to help us at those times. She has the keys to unlock the obstacles that might try to stop us, and the torch to light our way until we re-emerge anew on the other side.

CHAPTER 6
LILITH

After Yahweh created the world, he used the clay in the soil to create the first two humans: the man, Adam, and the woman, Lilith. Yahweh put the two humans in the garden of Eden and instructed them to multiply so as to populate the earth.

Problems soon arose when Adam tried to subjugate Lilith, especially during sexual intercourse. He wanted her to lay under him. She would not.

"I was made when you were. I am made of the same clay as you are. We are equals and you will learn to treat me respectfully," Lilith said. "We will come together as equals or we will not come together at all."

Adam could not accept such a situation. He demanded she lay under him. She refused yet again. In anger, she shouted the true name of God that should never be uttered. Then she flew up into the air and disappeared.

Adam could not live alone in the Garden of Eden and he appealed to Yahweh to help him to bring Lilith back. Yahweh sent three angels to look for Lilith: Senoi, Sansenoi and Samanglop.

They searched the world and finally found Lilith in a cave on the banks of the Red Sea. There she lived with demons and they enjoyed sexual pleasure together. She had given birth to hundreds of demon babies.

The angels took Adam to where Lilith was living.

"You must return with me," he demanded. "We are meant to live in the Garden, we are meant to procreate and populate the world from our offspring."

"Never," she said. "You cannot treat me as an equal and I will not be treated as anything less."

Adam became furious. "If you don't return with me, I will make sure a hundred of your demonic babies will die each day."

Still she refused. She vowed if he carried out his threat, she would kill his children in retaliation for what he was doing to her.

The three angels returned to Lilith. They knew now how dangerous she could be. They attempted to drown her. When she was near her last breath, they made a deal with her. They would let her live if she agreed not to kill Adam's children if they wore amulets on which one of the three angels' names were written. She agreed and her life was saved. She went back to her cave near the Red Sea.

Still, Adam needed a wife. He and Yahweh knew not to make the same mistake again. This time they made the woman, Eve, from one of Adam's ribs. The issue of equality would no longer be a problem, Eve was a part of Adam, owned by him. In this way he would have control over her and she would be a compliant wife unlike Lilith.

THE HISTORY OF THE LILITH

Though Lilith comes from Jewish folklore, it is thought that she appeared even earlier, as a Sumerian succubus, or a woman who appeared in men's erotic dreams.

In the Bible, in Genesis 1:27, there is also mention of the first woman made from the clay in the soil, just as Adam had been made. This is mostly ignored in Christianity and the story of Eve, made from the rib of Adam, is the widely told creation story. A compliant woman able to be controlled by Adam is the religious base from which much of the entrenched inequality between men and women in Christianity evolves. Since the subjugation of women by men is right there in the holy text, it must have been as God wanted—*or was it?* The writers of these holy books, both the Bible and the Talmud, decided to ignore the story of Lilith because they were men who wanted to promote the story that best served them.

Lilith is a highly contested subject among Jewish religious scholars, feminists, academics and many others. Some say she was not Adam's wife but instead his mother. For others, she has no role in the Garden of Eden at all, she is instead the Queen Demon. Others believe she is responsible for still births and babies who die of crib death. Boy babies are at risk of being killed by Lilith until eight days after birth when they are circumcised, an important ritual in the Jewish faith. Girl babies are at risk for the first twenty days of their lives. Lilith is also the cause of men having ejaculations at night, for their masturbation, and for their erotic dreams, not the men themselves, or so these people believe.

Feminists have long seen Lilith as not only the first woman, but the first feminist. They have embraced her for refusing to be controlled and subjugated by Adam and the angels sent by God. She also took control of her sexuality and proudly embraced it, something nearly all religions deprive women of. In fact, Jewish feminists so love Lilith, their feminist magazine is called *Lilith*.

LILITH'S LESSONS FOR US

It is clear that Lilith is a dark goddess with important lessons for us. She knew who she was and she would not be subservient. She recognized that she was equal to Adam. Against incredible resistance, she stood in her true self. Despite protests from Adam, the three angels, and even Yahweh, she would not give in. She was not willing to swallow her truth so as to be the "good woman" God and Adam wanted her to be.

She teaches us that we are equal. We deserve to be treated equally and when we are not, we still must stand our ground. Society and, indeed, these religions have engaged in a long, unrelenting battle to push women into the place they have defined for them, the place that serves *them,* not us. Lilith teaches us to refuse to be compliant, refuse to accept their inaccurate definition, to be certain of who we are and from where we have come.

It is right for us not to conform. If who we are does not sit well with whatever society, culture or religion wants us to be, Lilith teaches us that it's fine. We must be who we are. The world will know what to do with that. Our job is to be who we are and not to allow ourselves to be bullied by anyone, even someone as mighty as God.

We already know that our shadow is full of the parts of us that our ego does not want the world to see. Our ego has not learned Lilith's lessons. We must fight against its bullying and reclaim our true parts from the depths of our shadow, no matter how nonconforming they might be, no matter how society might judge them.

The other important lesson that Lilith teaches us, especially women, is that our sexuality is an integral part of who we are and we have the right to claim it as such. In fact, to not do so is an injustice to ourselves. In this world, when it comes to sexuality for women, we are offered either the Madonna or the whore. The truth about our sexual side is hidden deep in our shadow.

Lilith was not willing to deny her sexual side, and we can no longer deny it either.

Women, just like men, are sexual beings. We can only be complete when we embrace every aspect of our sexuality and act on it. Women are not meant to be a receptacle of men's sexuality and desires, to be some sort of compliant toy. Women have their own sexual desires and should never be ashamed of them, despite what society, culture or religion might try to dictate. Because of the enormous pressure against a sexually empowered woman, many women's sexual desires have been pushed into their shadow. These women begin to believe that they are not interested in sex and have no sexual desires, which is obviously aburd. Lilith wanted equality when it came to sex, just like in every other aspect of her life, and she gave up everything for it. She teaches us that women must be free to enjoy their sexuality in the same way that men are.

Lilith, the first woman, was an independent woman, subjugated by no one. This was unacceptable to the Hebrew patriarchy and as such she has been either labeled as a demon or erased completely. She is not a demon. She is a dark goddess with immense feminine power who can teach us valuable lessons. We can ask her to guide us to recovering the parts of ourselves we need to be complete once again, as we were always meant to be.

Symbols associated with Lilith are the screech owl, talons, wings, and the snake.

A RITUAL FOR LILITH

Requesting the guidance of Lilith on your shadow work journey should be approached carefully. She is a powerful goddess with transformative lessons. Be prepared to change.

This ritual has two parts. I advise setting up a quiet area in your home to create an altar to Lilith. The altar will be used over many weeks and perhaps even longer, depending on how you will require Lilith in your journey.

The altar should have the following:

- Red and black candles
- Onyx, moonstone or obsidian crystals
- Jasmine and musk incense
- A glass or chalice for red wine

Begin your request for guidance at your altar. This first interaction with Lilith, in which you make your request for guidance, should be done two weeks before the full moon.

What you will need for this ritual:

- Red wine (red juice if you do not drink alcohol)
- Black paper
- A white or silver pen
- A dish to burn in
- Rose essential oil
- Jasmine and musk incense

Sit in front of your altar. Pour wine into the chalice and light sticks of jasmine and musk incense along with the candles.

Rub a few drops of rose essential oil on your third eye and on your sacral chakra.

Sit in front of the altar, close your eyes, and breathe deeply to calm your mind. Now see Lilith. Think of the ways she might guide you in your shadow work. When you have decided exactly how you would like Lilith to help you, open your eyes.

Write on the black paper using the white or silver pen or pencil. Write to Lilith respectfully asking her to help you in a specific way. An example might be:

Goddess Lilith, I want to embrace all aspects of my sexuality and bring it fully into my active consciousness to become a permanent part of my personality.
May you be may you be my guide on this sacred journey?

Now set the paper alight until it burns to ashes. The message has entered into the ether. Lilith will receive it. Thank Lilith and drink the wine.

For the next two weeks, visit your altar to meditate each evening for about ten minutes. Light the candles and incense and clear your mind to allow for any messages to arrive. Note in your journal anything that arises.

On the night of the full moon, after it has risen, finish the ritual. By this time, you should have already begun your work on the part of your shadow for which you requested Lilith's help. You should already be feeling her guidance and wisdom. This full moon ritual is a gratitude ritual.

When the moon has risen, put on clothes that make you feel the power of your sensual self. Go out to the moon. Hold your hands out to her, feel the connection. Feel a three-way connection between you, the moon, and Goddess Lilith. Then chant the following:

My teacher and guide
Woman of wisdom and freedom
Lilith, our reclaimed first woman,
Goddess and Guide
You have helped me
You have showed me myself
I am grateful
I am grateful
I am grateful

Close your eyes, your hands still held high in connection with the moon and Lilith. Feel the gratitude for your transformation.

This entire ritual can be repeated the next month from the beginning to the end for a new issue in your shadow that you would like Lilith's help with.

EVOKING LILITH

For many of us, it does not take much effort to see how Lilith was treated reflected in our own lives. Some of the most harmful effects of our disjointed psyche are caused by our own denial of who we truly are and by conforming to avoid ridicule and rejection. The constant, never-ending pressure on us to fit into those regulated square boxes that should never house a free soul is often hard to stand up to. Even after we begin the work to release our true selves from our shadow, life will not stop. Society will not relent. This is why keeping Lilith, her myth, and her lessons nearby is so important.

One thing you can do to counteract the world's pressure to conform is to keep Lilith's altar as a permanent place in your home. Go there and call her to you when the world is attempting to tamp you down.

It's also always worthwhile to keep symbols of our goddesses on us. You might look for a small owl or a pair of wings to keep in your pocket or handbag to act as a touchstone to remind your psyche not to forget what Lilith has taught you and to prevent any regression on your journey. Do not underestimate the insidiousness of resistance to your transformation. It can pop up everywhere.

Lilith is a powerful dark goddess on our transformative journey. If we have been beaten down by life and society, pressured to be the "good girl" who is just like all the other good girls who follow the norms of our culture, Lilith is there to show us how to escape such a soul-destroying trap. We must reclaim ourselves and our sexuality, and reject all conformity that does not align with who we are, no matter how uncomfortable that might make those around us.

CHAPTER 7
OYA

Sango was an Alaafin, or emperor, of Oyo, a rich Yoruba empire. He was a powerful and fierce man. He had two wives: Oshun, his first wife, and Oba, his second wife. Even so, Sango was at the marketplace one day and saw Oya, the most beautiful woman he had ever seen. He wanted her to be his third wife, so he followed her home to Ira, a small town near Offa, in Nigeria.

Once there, Sango was shocked to see Oya put on a fur coat and change into an antelope and run away. He didn't know what to think about such a woman so he went to his oracle, Orunmila, for advice.

Orunmila told Sango that the antelope-woman was very powerful. "She control the wind and earth," Orunmila told him.

Sango was stunned that someone was as powerful as him and said, "But I must have her as my wife. Tell me what to do."

Orunmila told Sango that if he gave her fur, she would be his forever. "But she has a fierce temper. If she is angry, she can kill people and destroy an entire village. You must approach her carefully. She can be appeased with bean cakes."

The next market day, Sango arrived early and hid, waiting for Oya to arrive. After a while, an antelope appeared. Sango watched as the antelope removed her fur and transformed into the beautiful Oya. She hid her fur in the bushes and went to sell.

While she was gone, Sango stole her fur and hid it in a sacred room at his palace. When Oya was ready to leave, she could not find her fur, so she sat down and began to cry.

Sango appeared and consoled her. "What's wrong?" he asked, sitting down beside her.

"I've lost something very important." Oya looked at Sango and felt kindness and love for him, just as Orunmila had predicted.

"Come home with me and I will find for you what you have lost," Sango reassured her.

Oya went home with him and he found her fur for her. She was very happy and agreed to marry him, even though he had not paid a dowry.

Sango had inherited thunder-stones from his grandmother and was able to produce thunder and lightning. He soon realized that his powers and his new wife's powers could work well together. Oya would handle the wind, and Sango would follow with thunder and lightning. Sometimes Oya only cleared out deadwood with her wind, but if she was angry, she would use her wind to clear the entire village. She became especially angry at people because of deceit, dishonesty and injustice.

Oya became Sango's favored wife. He often took advice from her. And she was the only wife who stuck with him until the end. She advised him that his two most powerful generals could cause him harm. They were ambitious and might want to remove him from the throne. She and Sango planned to pit the two generals against each other in the hope of being rid of both of them, but unfortunately the plan failed, and Sango was forced to abdicate his throne. While his other two wives left, not wanting to be associated with a disgraced king, Oya stayed with him.

In shame, Sango hung himself. Oya drowned herself so as to be with him and they entered the afterlife together to become powerful orisha, or deities, together.

THE HISTORY OF OYA

Oya comes from Yoruba mythology. The Yoruba people live primarily in the southwestern part of Nigeria, in West Africa. In the Yoruba religion there is only one supreme god, Olorun, and all who are under Olorun are called orisha or deities, which is actually what Oya is.

Oya is also found in Brazil. Because of the trans-Atlantic slave trade, one often finds Yoruba words, foods, and religious and cultural practices in the cultures of people in the Caribbean and Brazil, where many West Africans were taken as slaves. Oya is the patron goddess of the Niger River, which is also called Odo-Oya (River Oya) in Yoruba. The Amazon River is also sometimes called Oya's River.

Oya is the goddess of transitions as well as the goddess of weather, in particular wind and weather systems associated with wind, such as tornadoes. She is particularly noted for being with people as they transition from life to death, during those last breaths. If she believes that the dying person has not completed what they were meant to on Earth, she can also stop the transition and send them back to finish their work. Because of her relationship with death she is the guardian of graveyards.

Oya is sometimes called Mother of Nine because, though she was initially barren or only gave birth to stillborn babies, she made an offering to Olorun of a sacred piece of rainbow material, and then gave birth to nine children, four sets of twins and a single child, Egungun. She's often shown with nine whirlwinds around her and nine is a sacred number in relation to her.

She is known to be very wise when it comes to business and trading and business people often pray to her for help in those areas. She is a protector of women and can help to resolve conflicts for them. She is a powerful goddess with psychic abilities. Oya is still worshipped today and people pray to her daily. They often make offerings of bean cakes during their prayers.

She is depicted holding a sword or a machete, which she uses to clear her way. These are among her symbols, which also include antelopes, wind and whirlwinds, a horsetail whisk, a buffalo and fire.

OYA'S LESSONS FOR US

Oya is seen by some as evil since she's associated with death and graveyards, and also because her anger flares and she makes winds strong enough to kill and flatten entire towns. But that's the wrong way to view her.

I think most of us fear death, especially that in-between place, the transition. Oya appears there to help the dying person, to calm them and make the passing easier. She is the goddess of transition. This is important when we speak about our shadow work. She can be there for us during those moments at the cusp of us releasing things from our shadow, some that we fear, most that will change us. In those moments, Oya can be called upon to alleviate our stress about such changes.

The important lesson that she teaches us is that for new things to grow and prosper, old, dead, unhelpful things must be removed. Her wind comes up when she's angry and she's angered by injustice, lies and deceit. And what is more deceptive than our ego? Our ego has decided who it thinks we should be. After we have been chastised and victimized, beaten and bullied into what the world wants us to be, the ego creates that person. All that does not represent this made-up personality in the correct light is banished to the shadow. But what is that person that the ego brings to the world except an amalgamation of lies and deceptions?

Oya becomes infuriated by this. Her wind can clear all of that away. She teaches us that branches and new leaves cannot grow on a tree full of dead wood. Before we can truly be the person we are, we must remove all the parts that we are not. This is imperative for us to make progress.

A RITUAL FOR OYA

Most of us, if we take time to make a personal inventory, know which parts of our conscious personality are not true, and are instead put in place to create someone more pleasing to the world. This ritual will begin to remove those aspects that do not serve you.

Think of a few things you would like Oya's wind to blow away for good. Write them on tiny scraps of paper. Try to use thin paper that will easily biodegrade.

Oya creates her wind by spinning her wide skirt. You need to emulate that. Put on a skirt, dress or wrap that can spin out from your body when you twirl in circles.

Take the tiny sheets of paper that you've written on outside. Stand in a place where you have room to spin in a circle. Take one of the pieces of paper, read it aloud and take a moment to think about that aspect of yourself. See it for what it is: an injustice to your true self. Ask Oya to take it away with her wind.

Now begin spinning. Make nine complete rotations for each piece of paper. As you spin, tear the piece of paper into tiny bits and let them fly away from you. Envision those no longer needed deceptions that live in your ego being cleaned out of you by the strong regenerative wind made by your spinning. When the nine revolutions are complete, stop and see that clean, empty space inside you where the lie was, which is now ready for new truthful aspects of yourself that have been hiding in your shadow. Repeat the spinning ritual for each of the pieces of paper.

This ritual can be done whenever one of these false aspects of yourself reveals itself.

EVOKING OYA

Each day we face issues in which Oya's spirit energy within us can be empowering. In the chapter on Jungian psychology, we learned about the archetype called the persona. All of us have personas we put on for different scenarios but also - importantly - take off. Occasionally these personas can get stuck, though. Evoking Oya's cleansing wind within can move them on their way when you realize that they are merely a tool, not part of who you truly are.

Take, for example, a husband and wife. Some men prefer their wife to be weaker than them. Some wives, though they know themselves not to be weak, and especially not weaker than their husbands, might put on a persona when he is around. They know this makes their husband feel better about himself and they love him so they do it or him. But when he's not around, they put away that persona, and can be who they truly are. Sometimes, though, they might get stuck, and if this happens regularly, they can lose their true self in their shadow and believe the weak wife is who they are. If you find yourself in similar circumstances, you can evoke Oya from within to stop this. If you keep a symbol of her with you, you can refer to it to conjure her cleansing wind anywhere. To blow that persona away so that your true self can come back.

Yoruba mythology is quite different from most European mythology, so you might also like to learn more about Oya by reading more Yoruba mythology. You might learn more about the parts of her that you feel are a part of you too.

Making the spinning ritual a regular tool to cleanse yourself of falsehoods will also help you recognize the powers of Oya that live in you.

Oya is a powerful dark goddess who can help us during the frightening transitions we must make when we do effective shadow work. She will guide you until you reach the other side. And her cleansing wind will make the unjust right by clearing out all the falseness that we've gathered along the way to protect us and cover our wounds. When we awake to our truth, we no longer need those things; they are merely rubbish taking up space. Oya will use her wind to cleanse everything.

CHAPTER 8
KALI

One day the Goddess Durga was set upon by two demons: Chanda and Munda. They'd been sent to attack her. At first, she attempted to reason with them.

"I've done nothing to you. Leave me alone!" she said, trying to be on her way.

"We will kill you today!" Chanda shouted at her.

They continued to taunt her and moved closer and closer. She tried to get away from them but they followed her, becoming rougher and rougher. She was getting angrier and angrier.

"I warn you to leave me alone. You will not like what the outcome will be," Goddess Durga warned the demons. They responded by laughing.

Finally, Durga lost all of her composure. From her anger-wrinkled forehead appeared the Goddess Kali.

The demons stepped back in surprise. Kali was fierce looking. Dark blue in colour, wearing a sari made of tiger skin. Around the sari was a skirt of human arms. Around her neck a garland of 108 severed human heads. Her small fangs at the corners of her mouth dripped with blood. Her four arms readying to attack.

Chanda and Munda called for their demon army knowing alone they were outmatched by Kali. The demon army appeared, but they are nothing up against Kali. She went through them effortlessly, crushing them to death and then eating their bodies. She ended by cutting off the heads of the two offenders who attempted to abuse the Goddess Durga, Chanda and Munda.

Just as she thought the battle was over, Raktabija appeared. The demon Raktabija had a special quality, if a drop of his blood touched the ground, an exact replica of him grew anew on that spot.

Kali began to fight him with her mighty sword she holds in one of her four hands. Each time he was wounded a hundred new Raktabijas joined the battlefield. Kali knew she must solve this problem in another way. She grabbed Raktabija and sucked all of his blood out. Then in quick order she ate all of his many copies around the battlefield.

All the demons were dead, the battle was over, and Kali had saved her beloved goddess Duga's life.

THE HISTORY OF KALI

Kali is a Hindu goddess of time, energy and destruction. She is the manifestation of the Hindu concept of shakti, a force composed of the primordial cosmic energy of the universe, which can be both constructive and destructive. She is also the goddess who can decide who deserves moksha, a term for various forms of emancipation and enlightenment. She is one of Lord Shiva's wives. Pravati, who calms Lord Shiva and tries to keep him balanced is his other wife. Kali, on the other hand, encourages Shiva's antisocial and destructive side.

The Goddess Kali first appears in *Devi Mahatmya,* a text of Hindu philosophy in the 6th century AD. She is depicted as a four-armed, fierce-looking goddess. In her hands she carries important items that assist in our understanding of her. In her left hands, she carries a severed head in one and a sword in the other. The severed head stands for the ego, the sword for knowledge. Our ego must be severed so we can achieve divine knowledge. The fingers on her right hands are forming shapes or mudras that represent fearlessness and blessings. They tell her worshippers that if they come to her in a true, fearless manner, she will be their guide to the afterlife.

Around her neck is a garland made of 108 heads. This is a sacred number in the Hindu religion, as it represents the universe and everything in it. It's also the distance from our body to the god within us, a distance of 108 units.

Kali represents the wild, divine feminine in all of us.

KALI'S LESSON FOR US

When Kali fought off the demons to save Durga, she was protecting the sacred against evil. Kali teaches us that our shakti can be used to create, but sometimes it must be used to destroy. She teaches us that anger is a destructive force, but it can also be a sacred one. Divine rage, the rage against evil, against demons, is important and necessary. It's the sort of rage a mother summons when her child is attacked. It is the rage that we must summon when what is important, what is sacred, what we love, is attacked. We must use that rage as the fuel in the fight that leaves no option for losing, because the battle is far too important.

The demons outside of us are often the easiest for us to identify, and usually the easiest for us to destroy. They might be an undermining boss who disrespects us. We can kill that demon by quitting the job. Maybe the demon is a physically abusive partner. It's difficult, but still we can get away, break up with them, divorce them, call the police.

Surprisingly, the demons within us are the most difficult to kill. They are even sometimes the demons that keeps us embracing the external demons, even though they are hurting us. The power of the internal demons is immense and they have wide-reaching tentacles into all areas of our life.

Within us all are demons attacking our true beloved self, the self that we need to protect at all costs. These demons might include negative self-talk, self-limiting beliefs about ourselves and the world, past attachments to people and events that hold us down, past mistakes that we are unable to forgive ourselves for, trauma and abuse that we believe we deserved, and relationships that diminished us, just to mention a few. We should be furious that such things stand in the way of us living the full, loving, authentic life we are meant to be living.

Kali sucked the blood from her demons. She ate them. She decapitated them. She did all of that to save the beloved. You must do the same to save your own beloved, meaning your true authentic self. We must kill those self-defeating demons within ourselves using righteous fury.

Also, Kali teaches us to direct our energy, or shakti, correctly. We should not allow demonic emotions to take over. We must kill them, too. Perhaps your best friend is marrying a great person, but you find your mind drifting toward envy and jealousy. Those are demons. Kill them. Immediately redirect that energy away from those demons and suck the blood out of them before the drops can be born again in you in other areas. Kill them, completely, and instead, send your friend a message of congratulations. Tell her how much you like the person she plans to marry and wish them happiness.

When demons within you are blocking the life-affirming energy you need, there are symptoms. You will realize that you have no creative energy; your creativity will be blocked off from you completely. You will deny your own rage and sadness. When asked if you're okay, you will say you're fine, when in fact you are far from fine. You'll be living a double life, pretending that your life is one thing when you know it is something else altogether.

Kali teaches us to step back, find the enemy, make a new plan of attack, and then implement. Kill the demons. Redirect your positive energy around the scattered bodies and begin your path to your true life again.

A RITUAL FOR KALI

Kali is not subtle. When we invite her into our lives, she will act. She loves passionately. When you call her out, be ready for her. She will kill everything that is attacking you. You might be surprised at who the enemy is and where you will find them. For this ritual all you will need is your journal.Sit comfortably and close your eyes. Breathe deeply in the calming way that we learned in previous chapters so as to clear your mind of any thoughts. Now see Goddess Kali. Envision her as your ally. She is battle-ready, waiting to help you.

Now open your eyes and write in your journal what you think your demons are, both internal and external. Write quickly without stopping. Once your pen stops and you can think of nothing else, put your journal to the side.

Close your eyes again. Think about the demons you wrote about in your journal. Think about how they are trying to kill your true self. Think about how they have no right to do that. Let your fury build. Think of all of the opportunities you passed up because your demons stopped you from exploring them. Think of the depths of love you might have reached if these demons had left you alone to be vulnerable and true. Feel the fury. Let it grow. Let it fill every space inside of you. Mentally fan it like you would a fire. Let it grow into a furious, raging bonfire.

Open your eyes and re-position yourself into a yoga goddess squat, which means standing with your legs wide, feet pointing outward, and then squatting as deep as is comfortable. Hold your arms above your head bent at right angles. Close your eyes again. Reignite that fury-fire. From your belly, release that fury as a deep, resounding roar. Breathe in deeply and roar that anger out again. Do this four times. With each roar, feel the anger spitting out of you like fire from a dragon. The demons that are attacking you are burned to nothing by your rage, by the sacred fury Goddess Kali has helped you find inside of yourself.

Doing this ritual regularly is a good, healthy way to keep that flow of furious energy in your body productive instead of destructive.

EVOKING KALI

Maintaining and cultivating the power that Kali has taught you lives within can be one of the most useful tools in your shadow work and your psychic transformation. For women especially, who are taught that all anger is a bad thing, learning to find productive fury within to help you rid yourself of those negatives in your shadow can be a transformative thing on its own.

A very good way to keep Goddess Kali at the front of your mind is through journaling. You can journal in two different ways. The first is to talk directly to Kali. Ask her the questions you want answers to by writing them in your journal as if you're writing her a letter.

For example:

- Goddess Kali, what do you want me to learn?
- What am I suppressing that is bad and evil for my true self?
- Where can I find you working inside of me?
- What demons must I kill immediately?

The second way to evoke Kali with your journaling is by using your journal for self-awareness.

For example:

- What are instances in my life when I am angry but I smile?
- Why am I doing that?
- What have I not done in my life because I thought I could not do it?
- Have I *ever* felt my wild feminine self? When?

Ask yourself these questions. The search for the answers within will help you find the demons that you and Goddess Kali will kill to protect your beloved one, your whole self, and to bring her out of the darkness where she should never have been in the first place.

At first glance, the frightening Goddess Kali looks like a goddess we should avoid, with her bloody mouth and her neckless of severed heads. But she teaches us that our divine feminine self must encompass anger, sacred fury, and the ability to kill all demons that attack those we love. We must love our true self, the self that is hiding away in our shadow, enough to wage an all-out war on anything that prevents us from discovering and reinstating our true, beloved whole self to its rightful place.

CHAPTER 9
BABA YAGA

From Russian folklore comes Vasilisa the Beautiful, who lived happily with her mother and father. But then her mother became gravely ill. Before she died, she called Vasilisa to her bedside and gave her a small wooden doll. "Keep this doll with you always and never show it to anyone, and no misfortune will befall you. When you need help or advice, feed it and after it has eaten it will help you and keep you safe."

Vasilisa's father soon married again and her step-mother arrived with two daughters. Vasilisa's step-mother and stepsisters were deeply envious of poor Vasilisa because she was the fairest maiden in all the land, so they made her do all the housework hoping she would grow thin and ugly, and her skin would become weathered by the sun. But to their great surprise, even though they sat in comfort while Vasilisa did all of the work without complaint, she became more and more beautiful while their spite caused them to become thinner and uglier.

In fact, Vasilisa had fed her little doll and asked it for help, so the doll always helped her quickly finish whatever work she was given.

As she grew, the most sought-after men in the village came asking for the beautiful Vasilisa's hand in marriage. This enraged her stepmother and her stepsisters, so when her father went away on a trip, her stepmother moved them all to a gloomy hut on the edge of a dense forest, where lived the fearsome Baba Yaga, who ate men as if they were poultry. One evening, the stepmother and the three daughters were weaving and spinning beside the fireplace, when the stepmother put out the fire and went to bed, leaving only a single candle by which the maidens could finish their work. Vasilisa's stepsisters devised an evil plan and secretly snuffed out the candle, telling Vasilisa they needed light to finish their work and sending her into the forest to the witch Baba Yaga's house to ask for a new flame.

They knew Baba Yaga ate people and hoped they would never see Vasilisa again.

Vasilisa was very frightened when she saw the dense, black darkness of the forest, but still she found the courage to enter. She was surprised when three different horsemen passed her. The first was dressed all in white and rode a white horse. He was accompanied by daybreak. The second was dressed in red and rode a red horse. He was accompanied by the sunrise. The last horseman arrived only when Vasilisa stood in front of the fence that surrounded Baba Yaga's hut. He was dressed all in black, and rode a black stallion, bringing the night with him. He disappeared when Vasilisa reached the gate.

Vasilisa trembled with fear when she saw that the fence had been made with human bones, each pillar topped with a human skull. The latch on the gate was a human jaw. Baba Yaga's hut stood on four chicken legs, and instead of the lock was a mouth with sharp teeth. Suddenly from out of the forest behind her came an old woman, flying inside of a mortar that she moved with a pestle. In her other hand was a broom she used to sweep away the tracks left behind her.

"Who goes there?" the old woman demanded, as she climbed out of her mortar.

Vasilisa bowed and said, "I am Vasilisa. I've been sent to ask you for a flame. Ours has gone out."

Baba Yaga was very tall and thin, with a long nose made of iron. "Very well, work for me and I will give you fire. Otherwise I will eat you."

As they entered the hut, a birch tree tried to lash at Vasilisa but Baba Yaga stopped it. Then a dog appeared growling and ready to bite, but one word from Baba Yaga and it calmed itself. Finally, a cat appeared from the darkness, its sharp claws ready to scratch Vasilisa. Baba Yaga chased it off and said, "Do you see that once you enter my hut, if I don't want you to leave, it will be very difficult for you to do so?"

"Yes, I see that," Vasilisa nodded. Still, she entered the hut.

Baba Yaga gave Vasilisa a list of chores. Vasilisa and her doll went to work and in a short while the chores were finished. Baba Yaga was impressed, not only by the speed in which the chores had been done, but also at how carefully the girl had completed them. She took a long stick and plucked one of the human skulls from her fence. She placed the skull on the stick and the eyes started to glow brightly, turning night into day.

"This will guide you home and light your fire when you get there," Baba Yaga said. Her eyes shown with a knowledge that Vasilisa didn't understand. "This torch will guide you to exactly where you need to be."

Vasilisa thanked Baba Yaga and went home.

The stepmother and her daughters were shocked to see Vasilisa. They'd been sure they would never see her again. They rushed out to her to take the flame, but as the skull's eyes landed on each of them, they were burned to cinders.

With her stepmother and stepsisters gone, Vasilisa could return to her happy, peaceful life again, and await her dear father's return.

THE HISTORY OF BABA YAGA

Baba Yaga comes from Eastern Europe. Stories about her have been part of the Slavic oral tradition for centuries. There are thousands of stories about Baba Yaga. The story *Vasilisa the Beautiful* is one of the most popular and well-known fairy tales.

Baba Yaga first appears in the written record, though, in 1775, in a book by Mokhail V. Lomonosov titled *Rossi-ikaia grammatika* (Russian Grammar). The book compared Slavic gods to Roman gods, discussing the equivalent of each from each culture's mythology. But Baba Yaga had no Roman equivalent; she was completely unique.

Baba Yaga flies through the air in her mortar, rowing it with her pestle and sweeping away the tracks behind her. She lives in the deep dark forest and has all the knowledge of the forest. She has mirrors that can become lakes and combs that can become forests. She is of another world, but also lives in this one. She resides on the boundary between life and death. She is a strict grandmother who has all the wisdom of the world, and will eventually help you, once you have proven that you deserve her assistance.

Originally Baba Yaga was a goddess who controlled time, life, death and the elements. The three horsemen in Vasilisa's story are Baba Yaga's servants: Dawn, Sunrise and Night. She was powerful and embraced her anger and nastiness as part of that power. Because of this, over time our goddess has been transformed, and she's now depicted more and more as an old, ugly woman. A woman who eats people, though in no story does she actually do that. Some even find parts of her, such as her breasts and vagina, repulsive. She is "banished" to the deep forest for her audacity. The patriarchy responded to the original Baba Yaga stories as it does to everything it deems empowering of feminine energy. The patriarchal arms of society changed a powerful goddess into what they would call an ugly crone. We must reclaim her and all that she can offer us through her ancient knowledge.

Baba Yaga is the wild, free woman of the forest who knows the secrets held in the trees and plants. She is at one with the seasons and the cycles. In some stories she even shape shifts into a snake or a bird. She holds ancient wisdom and is an excellent guide for anyone willing to show their worth to her.

Baba Yaga's symbols include birch branches, mortar and pestle, and a broom.

BABA YAGA'S LESSONS FOR US

Baba Yaga teaches us that knowledge and wisdom can come from unexpected places and we must be open to it even if we fear where we are going. Vasilisa never imagined when she came upon this wild, magic woman in the forest that it would change her life, but it did. She was open to what Baba Yaga offered her. Dark goddess Baba Yaga also teaches us to trust our intuitions and face our fears, to be courageous when afraid.

In our lives we often come upon situations where we are frightened and we hesitate. Something inside of us says, "Go! Take that step!" But instead of listening to our intuition, we bow down to the external voices; society's power that keeps us where we are through fear. We don't listen to our own intuition even though we know we are the only ones who truly understand what we need. When we do that, we miss the opportunities that the universe offers us.

Imagine if Vasilisa had stopped at the edge of the dark forest and returned home because of her fear. She would have never received the gift that Baba Yaga had for her, the gift that would change her circumstances and allow her to return to the life she deserved.

We are here on Earth to learn; to learn what is both outside of us and what is within. Our teachers come in many forms. We all know it is not only the easy, good things that teach us lessons. Think back on your own life. What experiences have taught you the most? I think most of us will find that it was a struggle of some kind that first made us fearful that offered some of the most valuable life lessons.

To genuinely progress in our shadow work, we must trust our intuition. Fear will always be present, but we must ignore it and step into that darkness to learn what we must. We need to be ready to see who our teachers are. Baba Yaga has much to offer us about the natural world, the cycles on Earth and in the universe that have a profound effect on us, the power of our productive anger, and the ability we have to show our worthiness to receive our gifts—but also, our ability to demand others show us their worthiness.

A RITUAL FOR BABA YAGA

We need to bring Baba Yaga closer to us when we have been banished in some way for being our true selves. You will need her to help you kill your fears about following your intuition and turning away from society's rules and judgments that go against who you are. She will guide you to your truth and help you stand against anyone who wants to force you to deny yourself.

Baba Yaga is a stern taskmaster, though, and first you must prove to her that you are worthy of her guidance.

As such, this ritual has two parts. The first is for you to prove your worthiness, the second to ask for her help, for her to be your guide—for her to offer you the light for your journey.

The First Part of the Ritual

For the first part of this ritual, you must perform some "chores" for Baba Yaga. You will need to collect branches from a birch tree. The further you have to go to collect these, the better. Once you have the birch branches, lay them parallel in an open space in your garden in a way to prepare a sort of mat.

You will also need a mortar and pestle. Place it in the middle of the birch branch mat. Put rock salt in the mortar. The larger the rock salt the better. Now grind it. Envision Baba Yaga watching you. She wants the salt as fine as possible. It will be up to you to know when to stop. You must prove to her that you are worthy of her guidance so be sure to make the salt as fine as possible.

When you're finished, carefully sprinkle the salt all around the birch branch mat. Each time you drop some salt, see Baba Yaga. Envision her being pleased with your work. When you've finished, sit comfortably on the mat and meditate on the issues you would like Baba

Yaga to help you with. Keep the birch branches that you used to build the mat.

Between the end of this ritual and the beginning of the next one, write daily in your journal about the issues you want Baba Yaga's assistance with. Keep those issues near the front of your mind while you wait for Baba Yaga to decide if she will help you. What does your intuition tell you about these issues? List your fears about them. Ready yourself for Baba Yaga's help.

The Second Part of the Ritual

This ritual should take place when the moon is waning. Prepare an altar in your home for Baba Yaga. Cover the small table with either a black, red or white cloth. Put some of the birch branches in a bucket or large vase and keep it and the mortar and pestle nearby. You will need the following:

- Sandalwood and pine incense
- Vodka and glass
- Red, white and black candles

Light the candles and the incense. Pour a small amount of vodka in the glass. Sit comfortably. Clear your mind with calm breathing.

Close your eyes. Envision Baba Yaga. She has come to help you. You have showed her your worthiness and she respects that. Ask her to guide you. Think of the issues you would like her to help you with. Then repeat:

Wise woman of the forest,
I'm asking for your help.
Wise woman of the forest,
Goddess Baba Yaga,
I am grateful for your wisdom and guidance.

Repeat the chant five times. Then see Baba Yaga in your mind's eye. She is reaching out her hand to you. Take it. Follow her. Watch where she takes you. When the journey is over, pour the vodka over the birch branches and thank Baba Yaga for her assistance.

EVOKING BABA YAGA

We all need to have a Baba Yaga within, especially as we grow older. We gain wisdom from our experiences throughout the time we have on Earth. This is valuable knowledge. We should all be respected and honored for that knowledge. In our society that worships the young as the only place beauty can be found, we need to conjure our Baba Yaga to remind those around us to be worthy of our wisdom, exceptional worth and beauty.

As with most goddesses, keeping Baba Yaga's symbols around you will help: her mortar and pestle, her broom. You could also take to wearing her colors: red, white and black. Spend time in wild places, be still and listen. Let her come to you there from within. Feel your power. Take a moment to gather your wisdom in a single place in your mind's eye and have gratitude for it.

Baba Yaga is a goddess who responded to conformity with rage. A woman who defined her life on *her* terms and forced all others to obey or be denied her help. She did as we all should. She defined the worth of feminine power that comes in many forms and taught others how to respect it. Objects that brought others fear or revulsion like skulls and human bones, she embraced, to show us that fear was merely a lack of courage and commitment to one's intuition. She did this to teach us to walk within and through our fears, in order to find the gifts the universe is offering us.

CHAPTER 10
PERSEPHONE

Persephone was a young beautiful girl, the daughter to the gods Zeus and Demeter. One day she was out with her friends collecting flowers. She drifted to a field covered in beautiful yellow narcissus flowers. As she was picking flowers and putting them in her basket, a powerful man emerged from a crack in the ground. He drove a golden chariot. Persephone was very impressed by the man.

"Good afternoon, Persephone," the handsome, powerful man said. She was surprised he knew her name. "I'm Hades, the King of the Underworld. I've been watching you for some time. You're very beautiful, I'd like you to come with me and be my wife and become the Queen of the Underworld."

Persephone was flattered by this man. They talked for a while and soon she found herself falling in love with him. She thought about her mother, Demeter, and how she was very overprotective and controlling. She loved her very much, but she would also like to have some control and freedom in her life. Hades promised that they would rule the Underworld together. Persephone agreed to go with him.

When Demeter found that Persephone had disappeared, her grief was unbearable. She missed her daughter desperately. She searched the world over but to no avail. Demeter was the Goddess of Fertility and while she grieved her daughter leaving her, all fertility stopped. The crops died and the people became hungry and began to starve to death.

Zeus could not allow the people to die. He knew his daughter was with Hades. He sent Hermes to tell Hades that as long as Persephone had not eaten anything in the Underworld, she must be returned to earth and her mother.

Hades and Persephone listened to Zeus's message delivered by Hermes. Hades held out his hand with six pomegranate seeds on it. "It is up to you what you want to do, my queen."

Persephone ate the six seeds.

When Zeus heard what had taken place, he instructed Hades and Persephone that since she had eaten six seeds, she would spend six months in the Underworld, and six months on earth with her mother.

And so it was that when six months passed, Persephone emerged from the Underworld. When she did, her mother was overjoyed. That joy spread out over the land and the trees grew new fresh leaves, the flowers blossomed in a multitude of colors, and the grain grew tall and healthy. Persephone's time spent on earth each year became the seasons of spring and summer.

The problem came when Persephone needed to return to her husband in the Underworld. Demeter's sadness overtook her once her daughter was gone. In response to her sadness, the trees' leaves shrivelled and died, falling to the ground. The flowers lost their petals and turned brown. The world went into hibernation waiting for Persephone to return. The six months that she was gone became autumn and winter.

THE HISTORY OF PERSEPHONE

The original full, traditional Greek myth of how Hades and Persephone became husband and wife first appeared in *Homeric Hymn to Demeter*. The myth above is an adapted version of the Greek myth of Hades kidnapping and raping Persephone and stealing her away to the Underworld against her will. The retelling comes from feminist scholars who believe for various reasons that the original myth was an incorrect interpretation.

Patriarchal society could not allow a myth that showed a young woman having agency over her own life. Also, unlike all other gods from Greek mythology, Hades, though stern, was just. Though kidnapping and rape was rife among the gods in Greek mythology when they went in search of wives, there is no Greek myth in which Hades behaves that way. In fact, Hades and Persephone ran the Underworld together, equitably. In depictions they are usually shown sitting next to each other on their thrones adjudicating the cases of the dead together. In fact, their equality and loyalty and fidelity to each other is not found anywhere else in Greek mythology. It does not appear like a relationship between a kidnapper and his victim, which is why the updating of the myth seems important.

Persephone is split between her role on Earth and her role in the Underworld. On Earth she is the Goddess of Grains. She is often shown in robes carrying a sheaf of wheat. She's beautiful, her flowing blond hair often crowned with flowers.

But she is also the Queen of the Underworld, powerful and decisive. In other myths, she is the one who allowed Sisyphus to return to Earth and rejoin his wife, and allowed Orpheus to leave the Underworld to be with Eurydice. Persephone represents rebirth and death as she moves through her own six-month cycles.

In ancient Greece, both Demeter and Persephone were worshipped by secretive agrarian cults with magic, dancing and various rituals. Persephone's symbols include: bats, narcissus, pomegranate, grains, butterflies and Lily of the valley.

PERSEPHONE'S LESSONS FOR US

Persephone is a perfect goddess guide for shadow work, given her regular movement between the dark and the light. One of the most important lessons that Persephone teaches us is that no matter what is happening around you, you must not lose yourself.

In her life, she was pulled by her slightly over-bearing but powerfully-loving mother, Demeter, and the romantic love she had for her husband, Hades. The constant push and pull of these external forces, at first, had Persephone confused. She was young and didn't have the trust in her real, inner self yet. In fact, she had not even discovered her true self yet. She tried to please both of them, and let both of them control her. Until she went back into herself. When she did that, she discovered who she was and could then easily navigate these two powerful individuals and still retain herself.

Most of us have similar external forces pushing and pulling us, so much so that we lose ourselves. In these times, we can feel as if we've lost control of our lives or are barely keeping our heads above water. Perhaps it's children pulling you one way, a partner pulling you another. Or a career tugging you around when the weight of your finances pulls you elsewhere. Maybe it's emotions that seem to have you in their grip or past events and traumas that dog you relentlessly. Such powerful forces are easy to succumb to. In the midst of it all, we can become lost and unable to see our way forward. Persephone knows this, which is what makes her an ideal guide to show us how to get back to ourselves. To help us go into our shadow and find who we are and reclaim it.

Another important lesson that Goddess Persephone teaches us is to not allow our life to descend into victimhood. Unexpected circumstances are bound to arise. They'll knock your dreams and goals off track, in some instances they can knock you so hard you feel that you will never be able to rise again. You could let the emotions swallow you, and accept that you are a victim, someone with no power in your own life, who then allows those unexpected circumstances to control your life. Persephone refused to do that. Obviously, she never expected to be taken by Hades to the Underworld while she was out collecting flowers. But she did not allow herself to become a victim. She approached her new, unexpected circumstances as a woman with complete agency over her life. She trusted herself, and she trusted that she would find a way... and eventually she did! You can as well.

The last important lesson that Goddess Persephone has for us is that everything has its season. There will be time to be active, to get things done, to attend to the work. But just as important, there must be time for rest, recovery and replenishment. We must give ourselves that time. We deserve it. If we do not take it, we'll never be able to achieve the things we yearn to achieve.

One final point to keep in mind about Persephone is that she is the master of attending to grief, trauma, pain, loss, mental illness and anguish. She is the Queen of the Underworld so these powerful emotions are her daily work. If these are issues for you at the moment, Goddess Persephone may be your perfect guide.

A RITUAL FOR PERSEPHONE

Sometimes deities, including Persephone, may choose you. You will know this when their symbols keep reappearing in your life and in your dreams. In other cases, you will feel a connection with a goddess and want to call her to you with a ritual.

Persephone's ritual should be done during the full moon.

What you will need for this ritual:

- Flower petals, Epsom salts, and sweet-smelling herbs for an herb bath
- Four green candles
- Dark chocolate

- Pomegranate seeds
- Natural music of blowing wind or rustling trees

To begin this ritual, you must make an offering to Persephone asking her for her wise counsel. Once the moon has risen, find a patch of garden. It's best if it has flowers with blossoms or vegetables, but any patch of growing things can do. Take your offerings of the dark chocolate and the pomegranate seeds with you.

Sit among the growing plants. Feel their joy. Envision Persephone coming back to Earth from the Underworld. Feel the happiness of that welcome from the world around you. Place the offerings among the plants. Meditate on the reasons why you think Persephone's guidance could be so important to you. Meditate on each issue separately. And then with humility, ask Persephone to guide you with her wisdom. Sit for some time longer, clearing your mind into calmness.

Once you've finished your meditation, go in and run a warm bath. Put the Epsom salts, herbs and flower petals in the water. Light the green candles, put one at each corner of the bathtub. Turn on the nature music. Now step into the bath and relax completely, body, mind and soul. Let the healing powers of the herbal bath attend to your wounds inside and out.

In the days and weeks following, watch for repeated images or sightings of bats or butterflies, or any of the Persephone's other symbols. There might suddenly be more mentions of Persephone in your life in unexpected places. Perhaps her symbols will appear in your dreams. Be on the lookout for all these things. Write about them in your journal. The goddess is acknowledging you and offering her guidance in your shadow work. Listen to what she is trying to teach you.

EVOKING PERSEPHONE

Once you have established the connection with Persephone, you will want to keep it. One good way to do this is through daily pagan prayers to her.

In the night, before going to sleep you might say a version of this:

Beloved Goddess Persephone,
The night has come, the moon is risen
The sun is asleep
And it is time for rest.
I humbly ask you to protect me

Keep me safe and surrounded by love
Until the sun returns.

You might also have a daily morning prayer. Find your own variation, of course, as this is just a guide:

Divine Goddess Persephone,
You have brought me safely to this new day
And I am thankful.
Please be with me today,
Use your wisdom to guide me,
and hold my complete self in your loving wise hands.

You can pull Persephone from inside you whenever you are with the Earth and nature, these are devotional acts. Examples might include:

- gardening
- nature walks
- visiting graves
- meditating outside
- cleaning your family graves

Keeping Persephone's symbols around your house and with you can also keep her near. You might want to set up an altar with dried flowers, honey, crystals and green candles. Always keep your journal nearby so you can work on the lessons she presents for you. Like most goddesses, if she becomes your guide, she will present uncomfortable situations for you to work through. Journaling can help you understand how she would work through them and what that work reveals to you.

Persephone is a perfect goddess for shadow work because she successfully merged her light and dark side. But she is not an easy goddess to work with. You must remember, she is the Queen of the Underworld. When you call her, you will be entering her environment. Be fearless and she can help you make important, concrete changes in your life.

CHAPTER 11
HATHOR

The Sun God, Ra, was angry. The people were rebelling against his rules and behaving wickedly. Ra went to his consort, Hathor, to be calmed.

"Lie down my love," Hathor said. She massaged his body and they made love. She fed him delicious food and pots of wine. Still he could not let his anger go. This made Hathor quite annoyed.

She lay in his arms. She didn't like seeing him this way. "I will go to earth and punish the people for upsetting you."

"You are so full of love and joy. The people will welcome you as a gift not a punishment," Ra said, his hand on her smooth cheek.

Hathor stood and, in front of Ra's eyes, she turned into Sekhmet, a scowling faced lioness, the goddess of destruction. Ra smiled. This Hathor could indeed sort out the wayward people below.

"Yes, like this you will bring fear into the wicked hearts of the people."

Sekhmet descended to earth. Once there, she went on a wild, reckless killing spree. Her anger was unbridled, fuelled by her love for Ra.

Ra watched the destruction below. After some time he turned to one of his servants. "I fear she will kill all of humanity. But now I'm not sure how to stop her."

The beer maker stepped forward. "I have a plan."

He explained what he wanted to do and Ra agreed. "But be quick. Sekhmet will not stop on her own. We must stop her before it's too late."

The special beer was made. The beer maker's plan was to add pomegranate to the beer to turn it red in the hope that Sekhmet would mistake it for blood and drink all of it. Then he poured it on earth. He and Ra watched to see if the plan worked.

Sekhmet still wild with bloodlust, saw what she thought was blood. She quickly drank all of the beer. Soon Sekhmet became drunk and drowsy. In a few minutes she was asleep.

When she woke, she was calm and had transformed back into the beautiful Hathor. The killing came to an end and Hathor returned to Ra in the sky, again she was her kind, joyful, loving self. Now they both knew that she held both sides inside of her: the violent destructive Sekhmet and the loving, feminine, joyful Hathor. They were one and the same.

THE HISTORY OF HATHOR

Hathor was one of the most important goddesses in the ancient Egyptian religion, which lasted for more than 3,000 years. In one of their creation myths, Atum, the creation god who held everything in the universe inside of him, produced the first people—Shu and Tefnut—when he masturbated. The hand that he masturbated with was Hathor, which is why she is sometimes called The Hand of Atum.

Between 2700 and 2200 BC, the majority of the shrines and temples built in Egypt were for Hathor. She was the goddess of love, beauty, music, dance, fertility, love-making, cosmetics, drunkenness, and the protector of women's health, both mental and physical. At Dendera, 40 miles from Luxor, where the Valley of the Kings can be found, is the Temple of Hathor. The towering pillars once had paintings of Hathor but were defaced by early Christians, so are no longer there. Many of the temples to Ra, the sun god, and Horus, the sky god, her two main consorts, were also places the Egyptians went to worship Hathor.

Hathor was the mother to all pharaohs. Her maternal ways were often compared to the two other prominent Egyptian goddesses, Isis and Mut. Hathor's mothering skills were not seen as socially acceptable because of her uninhibited sexuality.

She is often associated with cows, which in ancient Egypt were symbols of well-being. She's usually depicted with a headdress with cow's horns and a sun disk in the middle. She will often be holding an ankh, the Egyptian symbol for life.

The duality of Hathor and her alter ego, Sekhmet, is referred to in an inscription found in the Temple of

Edfu, which says: "The gods play the sistrum for her and the goddesses dance to dispel her bad temple." The sistrum is an ancient Egyptian musical instrument made of a metal handle, often highly decorated, some-times made in the shape of an ankh, and has strings with metal rattles on them. It is one of Hathor's symbols and can be used to chase away evil and attract good. Her other symbols include beer, cows, lionesses, cosmetics and the sycamore tree.

HATHOR'S LESSONS FOR US

In one story, Ra is depressed and lying around, feeling demoralized by his gods. To cheer him up, Hathor flashes her genitals at him. She loves her body and sees it as a gift to herself and to others. It is never something to be ashamed of or to find sin in. Making love is a cele-bration of that body.

The constant war against embracing our sexuality, especially women's sexuality, comes from nearly every corner, from our religions as well as our cultures. Women, in particular, are not supposed to enjoy sex. A woman who wants sex and enjoys it is deemed a whore by a society determined to push our sexuality into our shadow.

The same applies to women feeling joyful and uninhibited. Many of us are embarrassed to dance or sing, but music is an integral part of being human. So often, the messages we get from society are that joy and play are sinful rather than an important part of our humanity.

Hathor's uninhibited expression of her sexuality is an important lesson for all of us. Everything about her is full of pleasure. Beauty, music, lovemaking, beer—she is the goddess of pleasure. She teaches us to embrace joy, happiness, and pleasure.

Those of us raised within a Christian, and especially a Protestant ethos, where work is seen as devotion and pleasure seen as sin, might find Hathor anathema to our life's ethos. Your ego will insist that your work is who you are. A person who does not work is lazy and laziness is a sin. But why is work given such a high priority in our cultures? Are humans meant to merely work and work until they die? That certainly cannot be a complete and fulfilled life. But so often we're told that's what a "good" person does.

Hathor asks us to step back and carefully examine life. Life is not meant to be about constant work and suffering. *How could it be?* It's meant to be about joy, to be pleasurable. We should not feel shame when we are receiving and giving pleasure. We should not feel guilt when having fun. What sort of fractured and wounded society or culture teaches its people that to be "good" you must not partake in anything that brings you joy?

Hathor is the goddess that will help you reach into your shadow and reclaim your joy. She will help you laugh again, to enjoy music, to dance, to find your playful creativity. She will guide you to seeing your body as your hero and ally. So many of us are not *in* our bodies. We are disjointed and fragmented. We live in our minds. We see our bodies as a burden, not an asset. Hathor will help you see the folly in this thinking. She will guide you to see your beauty. She will help you banish all the 'wrong thinking' that has been a part of your life until now.

Think about when you were a child. You loved your body. Most of us, if parents did not insist otherwise, would have been naked all day. Our body took us places. It allowed us to play and climb and run and swim. It gave us joy. Somewhere along the way we shoved that joy into our shadow. When we did, our bodies became a source of shame and disgust. That is wrong thinking. We must reclaim the instinctual love of our body with which we were born. Hathor is the goddess who will help us re-integrate that body-love with our whole self, where it belongs.

A RITUAL FOR HATHOR

It will be nearly impossible for you to find a sistrum. Instead, design one of your own. It can be made from any sort of handle, as fancy or not as you like. Then find some pieces of metal to act as rattles; bottle caps would work nicely. Remove the rubber inside because it will dampen the sound. Make holes in the middle of the bottle caps. Then find a piece of metal wire. String the bottle caps along the wire and bend it into a circle. Attach each end to a side of your handle, either by pounding the wire into the wood or securing it with tacks or small nails. The circle of bottle caps should be above the handle. If you shake it and it makes a rattling noise, you now have your own home-made sistrum!

When you shake your sistrum, envision it banishing everything evil: evil beings, evil thoughts, evil feelings. See it attracting everything good to you.

In this first introduction ritual to Hathor, you will want to look your best. Wearing cosmetics was seen by both men and women as a form of worship in ancient Egypt, so since you will be worshipping the goddess of cosmetics, go ahead and apply some. Apply kohl or eyeliner around your eyes to show Hathor your devotion. Feel free to add any other sorts of cosmetics you might like.

Now, light your favorite incense. Apply your most lovely smelling essential oil. The room you are in should be filled with beautiful scents.

Sit comfortably in the middle of the dimly-lit room. Take your shoes off, leave your arms bare. Either use candles or put a translucent scarf over a lamp. Play your favorite music in the background. Play your sistrum along with the music. Stand and dance if you'd like.

Now, sit again and close your eyes. Touch your feet. Feel your feet. Feel your warm hands on your feet. Appreciate your feet. Massage them, show them your appreciation. Do not allow any negative thoughts about your feet to enter your mind. If they do, envision yourself making them disappear. Enjoy the feelings. Let them fill your mind, reminding yourself how important your feet are to you, how much you are grateful for them.

Now let your hands touch your ankles. Massage them. Feel how it feels. Welcome your body back. Let your arms wrap around you like you're hugging yourself. Feel the embrace. Feel your hands on your back. A hug is love. Feel your love for yourself. Feel your love for your body. Accept your body as a gift, for that is what it is.

Once you are in your body again, envision Hathor. See her dancing in front of you. Feel the joy coming from her. Let it enter you. Stand and join her. Hear your music and dance. Feel the music in your body, let it move you any way it wants. Feel all of the sensations. Banish all negative thoughts that may enter your mind. They are your ego trying to stop your love of your body, trying to prevent your joy in pleasure from leaving your shadow and becoming a part of your consciousness. Those negative thoughts are your enemy, kill them viciously as Sekhmet would kill them. Rattle your sistrum at them, banishing their evil ways.

Dance with Hathor, feel the pleasure that she is showing you. Feel it everywhere. Dance until the music ends. Then sit back in your comfortable seat. Smile. Let the pleasure resonate throughout your body.

Later, write about your experience in your journal.

EVOKING HATHOR

One of the best ways to evoke Hathor's power within you is to make a daily practice of looking at yourself in a mirror, seeing your beauty and acknowledging it. It's best to use a full-length mirror and it's even better to do it naked. Look at your beautiful body. Begin every day with daily affirmations about your love for your body and all that it can give you. Your body was never your enemy, that was a lie your ego was spreading. Banish it. Kill it like Sekhmet would kill it.

You can keep Hathor close by finding sex and your sexuality again. Experiment with your partner. With or without a partner, masturbate again. Learn about your orgasms. Journal about them. Rejoice in the joy that can come from your sexuality. It is a beautiful gift your body has given you.

Do things that give you pleasure. Make a list in your journal of everything that brings you pleasure, then start doing those things. When you are doing them, feel yourself doing them. Be only in that precise moment. You will feel the power of Hathor from within. If eating chocolate cheesecake is one of your pleasures, then do it! Enjoy every minute of eating that cheesecake. Banish all negative thoughts, kill them. They no longer have any role to play in your life. You deserve pleasure, joy and happiness. There is no guilt or sin in anything that you find pleasurable, as long as it does not harm another.

Hathor is the goddess who will guide us back to our joy. She will help us re-prioritize pleasure. She will help us dig out our body-love from where we buried it in our shadow, so that now we can be the complete person, both mentally and physically, that we are meant to be.

CHAPTER 12
PELE

Pele, the Hawaiian Goddess of Fire, was the daughter of Haumea, the Goddess of Fertility, and Kanehoalani. She had six sisters, many of whom were also goddesses, and seven brothers. They lived on Kuaihelani, a mirage-like island that floated above the sea. Pele was very beautiful but she had a volatile temper, and when she became angry, fires would start around the island.

"One day you will destroy our entire home, Pele," her father scolded.

As she grew, Pele became more and more beautiful, and one day she seduced her sister Namaka's husband. When Namaka, who was a sea goddess, found out, she feared that if she fought with Pele and angered her, Pele might destroy their home, so she asked her father what to do. Pele's father decided that Pele must be banished. Pele was given a canoe and she sailed out into the sea. Namaka followed her, still enraged about Pele stealing her husband, and wanted to make sure she could never return.

Pele stopped at a nearby island and thrust her stick into the ground to create a fire pit to build a home, but before the fire could rise up from the ground, Namaka appeared and extinguished it, so Pele could not stay.

The same thing happened at the next four small islands, where Pele attempted to make a volcano but Namaka stopped her. Finally, Pele arrived at the big island, Hawaii. She thrust her stick in the ground and the fiery liquid-rock from deep in the earth rose to the surface. When Namaka attempted to put the fire out, the two sisters began to fight, but Namaka was bigger and stronger than Pele, and she killed her.

But Pele's spirit rose up and she became a true magical goddess, living in Halema'uma'u, the lava pit at the top of the very active volcano she had made, Kilauea. She still lives there today and controls all the volcanoes on the island. Goddess Pele still has a wild, volatile temper. When she is angered, the volcano erupts. The lava burns towns and forests to ash, but it also flows into the sea and creates new fertile land.

THE HISTORY OF PELE

Pele is one of the most important gods in Hawaiian mythology. Even after Christianity came to the island, the people still worshipped Pele and left offerings to her. Even now when a person's house is devoured by one of the world's most active volcanoes, Kilauea, they accept it as an offering to their beloved goddess.

There are many myths and legends around Pele. One is Pele's Curse, which warns that no one should take anything from the island. If they do, her wrath will find them wherever they go. This curse is believed even now to such an extent that the National Parks Service commonly receives packages in the mail from tourists who did not abide by the will of Pele and eventually regretted it!

Kilauea's regular eruptions cause much damage. The lava flows over highways, homes and forests, burning them to ash, destroying them as if they never existed.

At the same time, since 1983, the lava from Kilauea, Pele's lava, has created 70 acres of new land in the sea off the southeast coast. So Pele destroys and rebuilds something even better. The land made from the lava is very fertile and in a remarkably short time what was black and barren is a new thriving forest.

One of the first plants that grows on the fertile new soil is the ohelo bush, from which come ohelo berries. The berries belong to Pele. No Hawaiian will touch them until proper prayers and offerings are made. They know what the consequences might be.

Pele tries to warn the people before an eruption. She might appear as a beautiful young woman in a red muumuu or as an old woman with a little white dog. Whoever sees her is responsible for warning people that an eruption is coming.

Pele is popular; she even has a volcano on Io, one of the moons of Jupiter, named after her. Her symbols include fire, obsidian, lava stone, rubies, coconut, and gin.

PELE'S LESSONS FOR US

More than likely. we have all felt overwhelming rage. That is the Pele within us coming to the fore. Perhaps we have been betrayed, or denied, or abused. The anger builds into a seething rage. But what happens then?

Most of us swallow that rage. We push it deep into our shadow because to let it out might be destructive, or appear antisocial to others. The problem is that suppressed rage is deadly. It has been proven to manifest serious illness. In fact, science today is showing us more and more diseases that are caused by suppressed anger. For example, illnesses that cause handicapping pain can be traced back to suppressed rage in our unconscious. In the West, there is a pain epidemic. People have back pain and neck pain, joint pain and wrist pain. And the prevalence of opioids to treat all this pain has led to an opioid epidemic. But much of this pain is the result of suppressed rage in our unconscious, in our shadow.

Pele is a woman with deep, wild emotions and she *feels* them. She keeps them in her conscious mind and acts on them. To be full, complete humans, we must feel our feelings. If we do not feel the so-called negative emotions like anger, we will not have the capacity to feel the positive emotions like love to the extent that we should. We need to feel all emotions intensely in order to be alive in our life.

So many of us have pushed our emotions so deep inside of our unconscious that we find ourselves living in a fog of non-feeling. We disguise this situation with words like strong or stoic, and gloat that we are brave for keeping our emotions at bay. It is not strong to hide your emotions in your shadow and walk around as if you have none at all. In fact, that is cowardice. You must be brave to feel your feelings—*all of them.*

Goddess Pele teaches us that we must feel our feelings, but we do not have to act on all of them. We can step away a bit. Feel that anger, that jealousy, that joy, and then decide how to act. Make a decision. Do not suppress anything. Do not push anything into your shadow.

Another lesson that Goddess Pele teaches us is that some things need to be destroyed completely to be reborn anew. She is not a goddess you evoke if you want subtlety. She will not allow anything false or harmful to remain. There is no room for reconstruction on the original foundation. Pele is about righteous fury. There are times when anger is not only all right but it is mandatory. She can show you when those times are and how to use your anger effectively to begin the rebirth. She is the goddess for destruction, but also magnificent creation.

A RITUAL FOR PELE

If you feel a pull toward Goddess Pele, it's best for you to create an altar to her in a quiet place in your home. The process she will take you through will need you to be close to her as often as possible. Having an altar to her will facilitate that.

Cover your altar table with either a red, yellow or black cloth. On the altar have red candles, a bowl or dish for burning in, and a variety of crystals, including obsidian.

What you will need for this ritual:

- Paper
- Water
- Pen
- Spoon
- Salt
- A glass
- Small obsidian crystals
- Cinnamon incense
- A hand spade to dig a small hole
- Orange essence oil

Begin at your altar. Light your candles and incense. Apply the orange essence oil to your root chakra and your crown chakra.

Close your eyes and relax. Let you mind carefully travel to an instance in your life when you became angry but did not express that anger. It should be a pivotal experience that has left you with emotional scars, something that haunts you. There may be more than one of these instances, so focus on only one for this ritual. Imagine yourself back in that experience and feel that anger. Then step back a bit to observe the anger in your mind. Use calm breathing methods to let the strong emotions settle.

Once you are calm again, handwrite a letter to the person who caused you to become so angry. What did they do? How did it affect you? Write about the experience without any filters. Be specific. Be as honest as you possibly can.

At the end of the letter write: "I will now be healed from this anger."

Close your eyes again. Let any emotion out that you need to. If you need to scream, scream. If you need to cry, cry. When you are calm again, set the letter on fire.

As it burns, recite the chant below as many times as you can.

Pele, goddess of righteous anger, heal me.
Guide me to release all hold this anger has inside of me.
I will be healed now.
I will be healed now.

When the letter is complete ash, take the glass and fill it halfway with water. Add salt to it and stir. When the salt has dissolved, put all the ash in the water and stir.

Take the glass, your hand spade and the small obsidian crystal outside. Dig a small hole. Pour the entire contents of the glass into the hole and let the earth swallow it. Then place the obsidian crystal inside, a gift to Pele for her assistance. Close your eyes and thank Goddess Pele. Thank her for healing you. Thank her for taking the wound away, for helping you to dissipate the anger. Bury everything. You may want to do a short meditation to calm yourself before ending the ritual.

This ritual can be repeated as many times as needed if you have multiple letters to write. Leave about a week between each ritual. Use the intervening week to meditate and journal on the issue that was healed during the ritual you've already completed.

EVOKING PELE

One of the first things you should do if you want to keep Pele at the front of your mind and in close proximity is to find some lava stone that you can wear, either a necklace or a bracelet. Keep it next to your skin. This is stone from a volcano and will ensure that Pele is always near.

Make radical self-honesty a practice. If you think something is false, dig at it until you uncover the truth. Silence and denial are the opposite of what Pele is about. Speak out, especially when you hear something you know is wrong. Get angry if you need to.

Once Pele is guiding you, you will begin to feel an opening up, especially in your creative side. She literally builds fertile new land within you. What will you do with this new land? You will feel the impulse to create, so follow it and keep following it. We are all creative people when we let ourselves be.

Don't forget to pay attention to your emotions during this time. Pele will help you pull things out of your shadow, things that need to be dealt with and destroyed. Never dismiss the emotions. If you feel scared of something that is coming, don't avoid it. That is what your ego wants. Your ego wants you to shove those wild, untamed emotions back in your shadow. Do not do it. Face them. Feel them. Examine the reasons behind what you are feeling, as well as the emotions. Decide how to deal with them, because hiding them is no longer an option for you once Pele is your guide.

Remember, feeling those scary emotions will open you up. It will make you vulnerable. We do not want to walk through our lives with armor between us and our life. We want to be in there. We want to experience every single thing. That is living as a complete human. Because remember, you will also feel the joy, the hopefulness, the exhilaration, the inspiration, the love. You will be fully connected to yourself and your life again.

The dark goddess Pele is about those wild, untamed emotions. She's about destructive anger and letting that destructive anger out instead of pushing it into your shadow. In our unconscious, most negative emotions, like sadness, resentment, and jealousy, are converted to anger. That built-up rage is toxic. It can manifest as illness and it can keep us fearful of expressing our true emotions and feeling them. Goddess Pele shows us that anger has a purpose and must be felt, never hidden. Anger can be destructive but that very same anger can lead to a beautiful, fertile rebirth on the other side.

CONCLUSION

The dark goddesses have been part of our collective unconscious for thousands of years. During that time, we have been taught that they are evil, wild, and full of sin. They are darkness and those who don't know any better believe we must only look to the light, because they fail to understand that dark and light *must* live together. We've been taught to suppress them, ignore them, and disregard them, along with any lessons they might have to teach us. In many ways, the dark goddesses are our shadow personified. They have been forced into silence and we have been injured because of it. Our lives and personalities are fractured by their suppression.

Perhaps you were not aware of these ten goddesses before reading this book. That's because society has made every effort to ensure that we are ignorant of them, just as your ego works so hard to make you unaware of your shadow. The dark goddesses are a bit like Pandora's box; no one knows what might happen when they are released. No one knows their true power or their capabilities.

But now you and I know that they are immensely powerful and when we release them from our shadow and integrate them with our consciousness, we will reclaim our power. Our fractured selves will be made whole.

With this book, we have begun to learn about these ten dark goddesses and the power they exert. Each, like Hecate, have held up light to help us find them in our unconscious, to help us use their wisdom to begin to fully know ourselves.

It is not by chance that you came to this book. It is not chance that you found guides here who now help you reclaim yourself from your shadow. You were guided here, just like you will be guided in your life by the goddesses you've found living within you.

I hope this book has been an introduction to the dark goddesses and that you will continue to learn more about them. Keep coming back to this book to practice the rituals and relearn the lessons. As we all know, life continuously throws up challenges and curve balls, which is why we will do shadow work for our entire lives. You might think you've dealt with a certain issue in your shadow with the help of a particular dark goddess, when suddenly life shows you that you have not. Shadow work is not one directional. You will go forward, turn left, go forward and then suddenly turn back and go back to where you came from. There's nothing wrong with that, it's the nature of this work. Do not be discouraged. One dark goddess' lesson may need to be revisited many, many times. That is perfectly all right.

My wish to you is that you continue to evoke the dark goddesses. Do not let the world, which is always trying to suppress our dark feminine energy, win. We must be our full, complete, integrated selves, not the fragmented, wounded, limping people who are blown this way and that by the wind because they have not yet met their truth. The dark goddesses take us to our true selves and when we arrive there, there is no going back.

We can be our own dark goddesses and the world will have to accept us as our beautiful, wild, authentic selves.

RESOURCES USED

1. https://en.wikipedia.org/wiki/Shadow_(psychology)
2. https://www.youtube.com/watch?v=cGQ7LSAQwo4
3. https://www.betterup.com/blog/shadow-work
4. https://www.google.com/search?client=firefox-b-d& q=Jungian+archetypes
5. https://conorneill.com/2018/04/21/understanding-personality-the-12-jungian-archetypes/
6. https://www.verywellmind.com/what-are-jungs-4-major-archetypes-2795439
7.https://www.harleytherapy.co.uk/counselling/shadow-self.htm
8.https://www.youtube.com/watch?v=SZ90jN2R9n8
9. https://www.youtube.com/watch?v=5udJgxOBrtk
10. https://www.youtube.com/watch?v=5udJgxOBrtk

11. https://en.wikipedia.org/wiki/
Self_in_Jungian_psychology

12. https://www.thesap.org.uk/articles-on-jungian-
psychology-2/about-analysis-and-therapy/the-
shadow/

13. https://www.thetoolsbook.com/blog//getting-to-
know-your-shadow

14. https://scottjeffrey.com/shadow-work/

15. https://aromagnosis.com/2020/08/17/shadow-
work-challenging-times-and-the-dark-goddess/

16. https://teaandrosemary.com/dark-goddesses/

17. https://www.religiousstudiesproject.com/response/
the-dark-goddess-a-post-jungian-interpretation/

18. https://mysticgenius.com/darknessisntbad/

19. https://www.youtube.com/watch?v=Ipay6WzPrs0

20. http://jungian.ca/fairy-tale-interpretation/

21. https://tarotpugs.com/2017/11/10/the-dark-goddess-
the-shadow-self/

22. https://www.thecanadianencyclopedia.ca/en/arti
cle/the-goddess-of-the-sea-the-story-of-sedna

23. https://en.wikipedia.org/wiki/Sedna_(mythology)

24. https://www.goddessgift.com/goddess-info/meet-
the-goddesses/sedna/

25. http://femalefortitude.blogspot.com/2013/02/
sedna-inuit-sea-goddess.html

26. https://visiblebreakthroughcoaching.com/sedna-emerging/

27. https://en.wikipedia.org/wiki/The_Morr%C3%ADgan

28. https://mythopedia.com/topics/morrigan

29. https://www.ireland-information.com/irish-mythology/the-morrigan-irish-legend.html

30. https://teaandrosemary.com/dark-goddesses/

31. https://www.patheos.com/blogs/johnbeckett/2018/06/pouring-offerings-to-the-morrigan-in-ireland.html

32. https://health.clevelandclinic.org/essential-oils-101-do-they-work-how-do-you-use-them/

33. https://medericenter.org/the-mederi-blog/anointing-with-essential-oils-for-spiritual-healing.html

34. https://www.thoughtco.com/greek-mythology-hecate-1526205

35. https://www.britannica.com/topic/Hecate

36. https://en.wikipedia.org/wiki/Hecate

37. https://www.thecollector.com/hecate-goddess-magic-witchcraft/

38. https://www.youtube.com/watch?v=umuW6CP779s

39. https://www.greekmyths-greekmythology.com/myth-of-hades-and-persephone/

40. https://en.wikipedia.org/wiki/Lilith

41. https://www.britannica.com/topic/Lilith-Jewish-folklore

42. https://www.youtube.com/watch?v=01guwJbp_ug

43. https://www2.kenyon.edu/Depts/Religion/Projects/Reln91/Power/lilith.htm

44. https://www.ranker.com/list/how-to-summon-lilith/jodi-smith

45. https://mywovenwords.com/2019/11/sango-and-his-3-wives-oba-osun-and-oya.html

46. https://www.pulse.ng/lifestyle/food-travel/african-gods-who-is-the-goddess-oya/q5gf7h2

47. https://en.wikipedia.org/wiki/%E1%BB%8Cya

48. https://symbolsage.com/oya-goddess-of-weather/

49. https://www.starmythworld.com/mathisencorollary/2016/12/4/shango-and-oya-of-the-yoruba

50. https://en.wikipedia.org/wiki/Kali

51. https://www.elephantjournal.com/2021/12/shadow-lessons-from-the-goddess-kali/

52. https://www.yogajournal.com/yoga-101/goddess-yoga-project-shed-light-shadow-side/

53. https://www.kalicollective.com/blog/2018/5-ways-to-invoke-the-energy-of-the-goddess-kali

54. https://www.hinduamerican.org/blog/heres-how-the-number-108-binds-us-to-the-universe/

55. https://www.britannica.com/topic/Baba-Yaga

56. https://en.wikipedia.org/wiki/Baba_Yaga

57. https://www.youtube.com/watch?v=
aS4VCxMeWQM

58. https://tarotpugs.com/2018/09/02/witchcraft-and-
healing-with-baba-yaga/

59. https://theawakenedoracle.com/category/shadow-
work/

60. https://en.wikipedia.org/wiki/Persephone

61. https://www.greekmythology.com/Other_Gods/
Persephone/persephone.html

62. https://persephonessister.com/2020/10/15/the-
truth-about-shadow-work/

63. https://k-oconnell.medium.com/how-to-work-
with-persephone-716fe333594e

64. https://www.youtube.com/watch?v=hoq3t_dzw-Y

65. https://teaandrosemary.com/persephone-
goddess/

66. https://egyptianmuseum.org/deities-hathor

67. https://en.wikipedia.org/wiki/Hathor

68. https://www.worldhistoryedu.com/egyptian-
goddess-hathor-story-depictions-importance/

69. https://www.spiritualityhealth.com/6-ancient-
love-goddesses-to-inspire-your-inner-enchantress

70. https://www.worldhistory.org/Hathor/

71. https://en.wikipedia.org/wiki/Pele_(deity)

72. https://www.steffansjewelers.com/blog/post/the-
legend-of-pele

73. https://joyreichard.com/spiritual-growth/pele-a-goddess-on-fire/

74. http://www.mythencyclopedia.com/Pa-Pr/Pele.html

75. https://www.nytimes.com/2018/05/21/us/pele-hawaii-volcano.html

76. https://www.djuna.co.uk/blogs/the-beadzine/lava-stone-meaning-benefits-and-healing-properties

77. https://www.hellanamaste.com/blog/tag/aries

www.ingramcontent.com/pod-product-compliance
Lightning Source LLC
Chambersburg PA
CBHW071356120626
46546CB00002B/710